A VICTOF

A VICTORIAN SOMEBODY

THE LIFE OF
GEORGE GROSSMITH

STEPHEN WADE

CHAPLIN BOOKS

Copyright © Stephen Wade

First published in 2015 by Chaplin Books

ISBN 978-1-909183-70-4

A CIP catalogue record for this book is available from The British Library.

Design by Michael Walsh at The Better Book Company
Printed by Imprint Digital

Chaplin Books
1 Eliza Place
Gosport PO12 4UN
Tel: 023 9252 9020
www.chaplinbooks.co.uk

'My only ambition is that someone in the dim future may speak half as kindly of me, as Hamlet, Prince of Denmark, spoke of the Society Clown of his period'

(From the George Grossmith *Birthday Book*)

CONTENTS

A Note on the Dynasty

The number of Georges among the Grossmiths is an endless source of confusion. Genealogy sites concerned with Grossmiths attempt to relate and explain the branch that may or may not concern the Grossmiths at the centre of each family tree. With this in mind, the biographer has to make it plain at the outset what nomenclature is to be used. I apply the following:

George the First – father of my subject (1821-1880)

George – my subject (1847-1912)

GG – George, son of my subject (1874-1935)

PREFACE

What is it about Gilbert and Sullivan that still appeals to us, over a century on? The wit of Gilbert's words and the beauty of Sullivan's music, yes, of course; that goes without saying. But surely there's more to the matter than that. There's a meaning in the operas, even a philosophy, that goes beyond their jokes and catches. And we get a glimpse of this philosophy, I believe, in an image which tends to flash into my brain whenever I think about Gilbert and Sullivan: a man, resplendent in the robes of some high office – be it First Lord of the Admiralty, Lord Chancellor, or, for heaven's sake, Lord High Executioner of Titipu – with a disrespectful, larky look in his eye as if to say, "Isn't it silly?"

And when I consider this image with all due care and concentration, I realise the man has the face of George Grossmith.

There can be little doubt that the popularity of the operas in their original London runs owed much to the personalities of the performers: George Grossmith, Rutland Barrington, Jessie Bond and all the others who had their devoted followers. And as the series progressed, Gilbert and Sullivan began to write specifically *for* Grossmith and Barrington and Bond and so on, suiting the material to the abilities of the performers. Gilbert recalled that when he first had the idea for what became *The Mikado*, he decided almost immediately that "As the principal character was to be a Japanese executioner, it was obvious that this part must be written for Mr Grossmith, and equally obvious that he must be represented as an exceptionally tender-hearted person whose natural instincts were in direct opposition to the nature of his official duties." Ko-Ko was tailor-made for Grossmith, and when any of his successors take on the Kokovian mantle, they are, whether they know it or not, to some extent also assuming some of the characteristics of long-dead George, the first interpreter of the part.

Because Grossmith was himself a humorist and a songwriter of real distinction, he was better placed than most to absorb and interpret the humour of the great Gilbert and Sullivan roles. But, for the same reason, he did not always see eye to eye with Gilbert, who, as the original 'stage-manager' (director) of the operas, was primarily concerned with ensuring his own vision was created on stage as far as humanly possible. Gilbert coached the performers personally and to the smallest detail as to how to speak every line, how to make every movement. It is not quite fair to say that he wanted his actors to be marionettes responding to his commands, and in fact he was quite prepared to listen to suggestions made in rehearsal, but he always held himself to be the final arbiter, and if he didn't like an idea for a new line or piece of business, it didn't go in. It is easy to see why a man like Grossmith, an entertainer in his own right who had been used to having his own head as to what was funny and what was not, would not always be happy to give way to Gilbert.

However, in spite of this, Grossmith remained friendly with Gilbert to the end – with, perhaps, the occasional interval of coolness inevitable when dealing with a man as volatile as Gilbert. They visited each other socially, and when, for instance, Gilbert referred to Grossmith in a letter as "that homuncule", this should surely be taken in the spirit of affectionate raillery. Even when Gilbert wrote to Sullivan that Grossmith was "a d—d bad actor" this should perhaps not be taken at face value; Gilbert had, after all, been known to refer even to his own libretti as "d—d nonsense." With Gilbert, affection often had to be read between the lines – he confessed that "the Englishman's desire to keep his emotions to himself is always strong within me" – and he sometimes expressed his friendship in insults which could easily be misconstrued. In fact he knew very well how much he owed to Grossmith for the success of Gilbert and Sullivan; and he had enough regard for Grossmith to ask him later in life to compose the music for their ill-fated comic opera *Haste to the Wedding*.

The two men had essentially different styles of humour. Gilbert saw everything from the standpoint of a man who has had a revelation of the fundamental absurdity of life but has never become reconciled to it. Every fresh piece of evidence renewed his outrage, hence the satirical tone of much of his comedy. But George Grossmith was resigned to the foolishness of human behaviour, and was able to transform it into the observational humour of his songs, skits and monologues – not to mention *The Diary of a Nobody*.

Grossmith never seems truly angry with the craziness of humanity, as Gilbert sometimes does; only, at worst, exasperated. After all, if we laugh at Charles Pooter, it's only in the same way that we laugh at ourselves; because, of course, we *are* Pooter. The Grossmith larkiness that survives in the traditional performance of his Gilbert and Sullivan roles reflects this, I think. And we are all the richer for it.

Andrew Crowther

INTRODUCTION: DOING A TURN

'On the stage he was natural, simple, affecting.
'Twas only that, when he was off, he was acting'

Oliver Goldsmith: 'David Garrick'

There is no shortage of pictures and drawings of George Grossmith. They all show a neat, dandyish man, small-framed and athletic, with scholarly pince-nez perched on his nose, and a sense of fun and humour radiating from him. The images convey spriteliness, vivacity and wit. Here is a man who will provide you with good company, someone who sees the glass of life half-full and works to keep it that way. Many of the pictures show him at a piano, and for decades of his life, that was the how the public knew him – as the self-styled 'society clown.' He became very rich on that image, and when interviewed by a number of journalists in the 1890s, he was very much the representative of what many commentators were calling 'the New Humorists'.

Yet, in spite of two volumes of autobiography, Grossmith remains in some sense elusive. This is because his wit and humour constantly bubble on the surface of his identity; we long to know what lies beneath the smile and the pince-nez. As with so many impressionist comedians and satirists, there is an alternative self somewhere beneath the fun. This is not to say that this book will insist on following the modern trend of digging for scandal or transgression. Quite the opposite applies: this is the story of something very modern – a celebrity. He was a star for Gilbert and Sullivan, and in some ways they moulded him into the celebrity he became. But paradoxically, his name has never been out of print in spheres quite different from the Savoy Operas: with his brother he produced the timeless classic of quintessentially English humour, *The Diary of a Nobody*.

He was not an absolute original: before him there was John Orlando Parry, and this influence will be discussed later; there was an established tradition of the piano entertainer, with patter, asides and comic songs, and George Grossmith was well aware of that. He watched Parry in performance and he learned. Then, as with all true masters of their genre, he added his own panache and sparkle and he was loved for it.

A Victorian Somebody aims to recount and celebrate George Grossmith's achievement, and that goes far beyond any superficial 'celebrity' in terms of any transient glory or adulation. He has a permanent place in the history of the stage and of English literature, despite the fact that his classic work has attracted practically no academic criticism or analysis until quite recently.

Such was the irony with regard to George's biography that Stanley Naylor, an actor and friend, devoted a whole book to George's son, and this was written to illustrate what he calls 'the art of savoir-vivre,' taking the notion of 'gaiety' in general (rather than the theatre of that name) and applying it to George (Junior) as he knew him. Naylor's book rightly celebrates the Grossmith who perhaps had the widest general media presence, but the great Gilbert and Sullivan star stood in the background, as it were.

A Grossmith biography therefore has to cope with an initial explanation of the three Georges. George I, the father of my subject, was first and foremost a lecturer; then came George II of the Savoy and of the piano entertainment; finally there was his son, George III, generally known as George Junior or sometimes 'G.G.' Yet even before George I there were Grossmith entertainers, as will be explained in the next chapter.

I need to define and explain George the Savoyard and writer now, to bring him out plainly into the light, before the events of his life unfold.

*

On 11 May 1879, one newspaper reported that there had been a Benefit Fund performance for 'Isandula.' They clearly found the real Zulu name of the great battle in which the British army suffered a humiliating defeat at the hands of King Cetshwayo too difficult to spell: *Isandlwana* being the name. The entertainment paper, *The Era*, noted that the concert took place 'at the Gaiety in the presence of a large and fashionable audience, which included their Royal Highnesses, the Prince and Princess of Wales and their family.' At the concert, George Grossmith's contribution was described. He 'excited further hilarity with his own comical and musical description of a picnic party at Burnham Beaches.'

At first glance, this is just one more report of a concert, and in the Victorian years, entertainment was everywhere and for everyone. But actually, in what we learn of George Grossmith, the son of a popular lecturer, it is an important revelation. He entertained the crowd and royalty, very much as in the Command performance at the Palladium, still going strong today. He had an ability to perform for everyone. George could sing and tell stories to the East End music hall clientele, and to the middle classes out for 'culture' in evening parties, at formal concerts, or indeed, as he had started doing two years before this Benefit, in productions of Gilbert and Sullivan operettas.

Here was a man who had the magnetism and populism of a Dan Leno or a Chaplin, and yet he could don a tuxedo, apply hair oil to his well-groomed head and tickle the ivories for classical buffs. He was, for decades, the man you could book for a provincial tour, a special occasion or a charity concert. In short, he was a great celebrity, particularly in the years between 1880 and 1900. These were the years which saw the decline of the kind of variety which had boomed in the music halls, and had seen the rise of serious drama, burlesque, individual comics, and musicals. One review, in 1880 in *The Daily News*, understood Grossmith's talent, after he had appeared in a 'matinee musicale,' feeling that it also had to explain the phenomenon: 'An entertainment forming a kind of compromise between the freedom of the ordinary music hall and the refinements of superior concerts was given in Willis's Rooms on Saturday...' and the review went on to explain, 'The programme consisted of songs, recitations, imitations of actors, and humorous musical sketches, the latter given by Mr G. Grossmith with a degree of versatility and vivacity combined with humorous fancy rarely found in the same individual.'

Here was a celebrity, the darling of the reviews and the new journalism for the print-hungry commuter class keen for an evening read or a twenty-minute bit of peace with the paper commuting to work from the suburbs. But his genius does not end with the piano and the comic roles at the Savoy. He was a literary star as well.

His one work of fiction clarifies the 'two cultures' – the dual nature of entertainment in the 1890s, the time of Grossmith's zenith of fame and status. The importance of Mr Pooter and George's great bestseller needs to be pinpointed here, although I will return to the book in Chapter Seven.

George Grossmith's Mr Pooter, in *The Diary of a Nobody* (1892) enjoys a pipe, a trip to a guildhall ball and the occasional séance; his world of entertainment is based on a culture of aspiration and this is created by a range of acceptable leisure activities. These have their limits, and one of the unacceptable activities is having the kind of fun his son, Lupin, enjoys:

> 'Lupin informs me, to my disgust, that he has been persuaded to take part in the forthcoming performance of the "Holloway Comedians." He says he is to play Bob Britches in the farce, Gone to My Uncle's; Frank Mutlar is going to play Old Musty. I told Lupin pretty plainly that I was not in the least Degree interested in the matter...'[1]

Pooter wants to be an acceptable member of the new middle class – those who were at the time living in the London suburbs and travelling into the city to work, generally pushing pens. This new class hungered for self-improvement. Pooter is anxious to do the right thing, and desperate not to make a *faux pas* in the 'best' company. His reading, his entertainment and his recreational activities are carefully considered. His tastes are middlebrow, and that is exactly what the accelerating new media set out to satisfy. Yet, he has no time for a farce; he would attend a Shakespeare performance or the latest serious play in town, but low comedy was beyond his cultural boundary.

In contrast, we have Mr Leonard Bast, in E M Forster's *Howard's End*. Here is a man of that same class of clerks, descendants of Bob Cratchit but with an enriched lifestyle and some leisure time. Bast is inspired by Ruskin and wants to improve through study. His disposition is to analyse and discuss, to read widely and absorb anything considered to be 'high' culture. The crusade to educate the working class, from the 1870 Forster Education Act and later legislation on elementary education, had given the writers and performers of the page and stage a new and enthusiastic audience, eager for the kind of enlightenment their 'betters' had always had by birthright. In Chapter XIV of *Howard's End*, Bast is eager to express his thoughts about books and ideas, and his gushing enthusiasm fails to impress the Schlegel sisters. After Bast's talk about three different books in half a minute, Forster adds this: 'Tibby, who preferred his comedy undiluted, slipped from the room. He knew that this fellow would never attain to poetry...'[2]

The Basts of the new world of the class of clerks and commuters wanted their entertainment, but with more than a dash of high culture. The dichotomy of popular and highbrow entertainment was to persist through this period. In Max Wall's autobiography, *Fool on the Hill*, he describes the musical entertainment in which his parents (music-hall acts) worked around 1900: 'The music hall was then predominant in the world of entertainment. There were plenty of "legit" theatres where the great star actors like Irving, Harvey and Tree could parade their talents, but for the common run of humanity the music hall was the thing.'[3]

The contrast between the two literary characters of Pooter and Bast presents an interesting dichotomy: Pooter cultivates a social self, making friendships and sharing experience; there is a place for popular entertainment in his life, despite his choosiness. On the other hand, Bast turns in on himself, yearning for scholarship and depth of knowledge, longing for the acquisition of cultural knowledge and accomplishments which are in categories very much in contradistinction to anything for the crowd, for the masses. Each wants a certain sensibility, but Pooter's is sufficient merely as a thin patina, something which is part of his appearance, whereas Bast wants to be the peer of Oxbridge men, to read and discuss philosophy and literature with a proper acquisition of the bedrock of learning such involvement requires.

In the two we have glimpses of the extremes of the vast spectrum of entertainment available to people in the late Victorian and Georgian years. Yet of course, the performers and writers who worked hard to meet these new needs and pleasures of the expanding audience were from very mixed backgrounds; many of them could pass from one very low level to more respectable ones, as was the case with the noted actress Adelaide Nielson, who was commented on by Colonel Frederick Wellesley (nephew of the Duke of Wellington) when he 'slummed it' in a drinking house in 1860, a place known then as a 'night house' as he explains:

' ... they were most of them situated in streets near
the Haymarket. One that I remember was called Kate
Hamilton's and another Coney's. The first was a very large
room studded with small round tables ... It is said that it
was serving here as a barmaid that Miss Adelaide Nielson,
who subsequently became a great actress, was first seen in
London.'[4]

There was always going to be a struggle to try to add a little 'culture' and refinement to the popular entertainments of London. The challenge may be seen in the early history of the Old Vic. The

Victoria Hall, as it was in the nineteenth century, reopened in 1880 after having a first life as a place for rough entertainment and drunken brawls. Lilian Baylis' aunt, Emma Cons, took over, and as Richard Findlater explains, Cons had to work with the London County Council in order to broaden her entertainment offerings, catering for more 'civilised' customers:

> 'Emma Cons and the Council did not want to deter,
> by too much uplift and Education, the possible family
> audience in search of good, clean music hall fun.
> So they presented variety 'purged of innuendo in words
> and action' (as far, that Is, as Miss Cons could tell). The
> clearest indications of her intentions were signalled by the
> programme, which carried in the first two years improving
> quotations from Shakespeare …'[5]

In the years between c1870 and 1900 there was a stunning range of variety available, and the different audiences, with very varied needs in terms of the social use of their experience and of audience reception, had a multiplicity of choices for a night out. An illustration in *The Daily Graphic* newspaper in 1890 supports this view, and depicts the sheer diversity involved: there is the Ballet Cecile offering *The Dancing Lesson*; Dan Leno as *The Railway Guard;* the Selbini Troupe of Bicyclists; negro minstrel Chirgwin, and comic sketches by the Brothers Poluski. We may add to this dozens of advertisements for classical recitals, so say nothing of amateur productions such as an entertainment given at the Kensington Town Hall in aid of the Metropolitan Police Orphanage and Relief Fund.[6]

In the last twenty years of the century, the immense diversity of popular entertainment reflected a massive audience, all wanting social entertainment. The 1890s were arguably one of the most gregarious decades in British history. A scan of the pages of popular journals indicates a society clamouring for collective work and play; the society was very militaristic also, and people loved to wear uniforms and to march in the streets; they entertained themselves, but also relished being entertained – being there when there was 'a good turn' in front of them. The recently discovered films made by Mitchell and Kenyon has a number devoted entirely to street marches and brass bands, showing a procession in a northern town, consisting of teetotal groups, the Band of Hope, the bands of apprentices, the Primrose

League and dumb shows put on by colleges and schools. At the same time, the working men's clubs were beginning to have 'clean' turns rather than bawdy songs and toilet humour, and at the turn of the century there was a boom in popularity of popular recitation.

Drama and narratives of all kinds were gathering in popularity at the same time. There were song and ballad clubs; the folk song revival was gathering pace, and every conceivable kind of performer was in demand. An insight into this world is seen in the publications of musical agents showing their lists of artistes. For instance, in 1904, The Premier Provincial Entertainment and Concert Bureau, run by Mr W H Elston of Birkenhead, produced a catalogue with pictures and PR statements of the artists on their books. Elston offered performers for every conceivable occasion, from oratorios and banquets to dances and garden parties. At the classier end of the spectrum there was Miss Evangeline Florence, with this description and CV:

> 'Miss Evangeline Florence, soprano, is a native of the United States, having been born in Cambridge, Massachusetts, close by Harvard University… She had the good fortune, early in life, to fall into the hands of Madame Edna Hall, one of the most skilful voice producers of her time. Miss Florence made her first appearance at Boston, in the opera of Marta at the age of eighteen. Something of a sensation was caused on that occasion…'[7]

Elston also catered for variety: he had Mr Will Horabin, entertainer, Professor Weber, the 'refined illusionist and ventriloquist' and Mr Edwin Davies, described as 'Of Mr Arthur Roberts' Vaudeville Company' specialising in 'humorous songs, musical sketches and recitals at the piano.'

We need to look deeper into the world of stars and celebrities, but also with the writers, agents and managers who made things happen. The years covered were the time in which working conditions, contracts, copyright and organisational matters also experienced a revolution, as professionalism became more widespread and brought with it a need for regulation, accountants and solicitors. There had always been celebrities, but from the first newspapers in the early eighteenth century, there was a gradual rise in the level to which awareness of both performers and the 'backroom' workers such as the writers and impresarios increased. The Regency period saw a proliferation of actors in the limelight, and also the arrival of the celebrity actress. Part of my area of enquiry here is the nature of the celebrity performer and the degree to which he or she became known to the audience.

From the 1880s onwards, as periodicals became more and more interested in mediating the personalities of performers, profiles and interviews of artists became more common, as in a feature on George Grossmith, known to most readers as a star of Gilbert and Sullivan productions, shows; here, to accompany a sketch of him at the piano, face tilted comedically, the anonymous writer notes: ' Very solid and eminently respectable in aspect is Mr George Grossmith's habitation in Dorset Square, Marylebone Road. The decay of stage bohemianism notwithstanding, one would have thought of it as the residence of a fashionable physician or of a Chancery Q.C. rather than of the "Society Clown"…' [8]

The name attached to Grossmith hints at the gradual process of egalitarian status here, of artists of all hues; the last years of the Victorian age and the next few decades saw this development, although of course there was still high culture; but the point is that artists of all kinds and backgrounds found themselves working before mixed audiences; the age of variety was just that – but in many different ways, not simply in terms of music hall.

Any account of people and events involved in this exciting time for theatre and for writers have to include the centrally important periodicals: it was the age of the literary and artistic monthly or quarterly, and in *The Idler* for instance, edited in the 1890s by Jerome K Jerome and Robert Barr, may be seen an approach to this reader awareness to such an extent that production values and content are aimed at creating a cosy sharing of light-hearted entertainment, with artists and writers having a special kind of attention. For example, the editors had a rolling programme of features called 'The Idler Club' in which both writers and performers joined in to contribute to discussions of set topics such as 'Is love a practical reality or a pleasing fiction?' Then there was the feature called 'Lions in their Dens' which cultivated the apparent homely familiarity of readers with celebrities. In the first issue of 1893, the great man himself, George Newnes, was featured. Here was the famous entrepreneur who had started *Tit Bits* in 1881 and who later established *The Strand* magazine in 1891. He became a book publisher in 1897 and later was MP for Swansea.

In some ways, these features were the forerunners of *OK* magazine – profiles of celebrities at home.

Finally, there are the genres themselves in this period. Love and crime were prominent, as always, but the genre we now think of as true crime was emerging in various guises, and when we recall that the impact of macabre crimes such as those of Jack the Ripper in 1888 and anarchist killings in the street were happening in these years, it is not difficult to explain why crime stories were popular on the stage as well as on the page. The writers and dramatists were often profoundly aware of the new criminological interests of the public, and representative of this was undoubtedly George R Sims (1847-1922), who had been hugely successful in the 1870s with satirical works, but who, in later life, took a deep interest in matters criminal and in social investigative documentary. His success as a popular dramatist was phenomenal; his melodramas, written with Robert Buchanan and staged at the Adelphi, were very popular and exploited criminal themes such as the evil gypsy at the heart of his play, *The Trumpet Call.*

If one brings all these elements of the scene together, questions about how the new audiences were accommodated and how the entertainment industry changed tend to be raised. Parallel to that is the story of the amateurs also. Lupin Pooter's acting with his pals was just as much a part of the scene as the 'Society Clown' comedy of George Grossmith.

One strand in the complex web of people, events and influences in this history is that of the reinvention of the artist; biographies and memoirs of the period by those involved in theatre repeatedly note that potentially any individual could become successful in the arts, at whatever level, and those who really aspired to be 'somebody' revelled in putting on the façade of being a personality. George Edwardes, the producer associated with the Gaiety and earlier the Savoy operas as Gilbert and Sullivan's box-office manager, added the second 'e' to his name as he was transforming himself from the Grimsby boy who had come to 'the smoke' to pass exams for military service and failed, drifting into theatre work through desperation but finding that he had found his metier by accident. Within a year of returning from factotum work with a touring company, he was a close friend of Mr D'Oyly Carte himself. [9]

In looking at the establishments, management and media promotion of performers in this period, one finds the entertainment business in all its rich diversity, and this adds to our knowledge of that bland, self-conscious and influential sub-culture of the Pooters in their recreational time. The world of entertainment c1900 was multi-layered and performers worked at every level, from readings and recitals to grand opera and serious drama. The writers who provided the material were working in an increasingly complex world in which professionalism was being created and defined, partly through the growth of intellectual property legislation. The performers existed, for the most part, in a designated slot within the very wide spectrum in the performing arts, both amateur and professional. As for the audience and readership, they were an identity in flux, eager for things to do after their long working hours and economic pressures.

Looking at the entertainment world and its contexts immediately opens up an understanding of the significance of the 1890s in terms of how we may understand the emerging literary culture based around a revolution in reading for the new commuter class, as placed alongside the milieu of the bookman and the 'new' author with his or her openings across the spectrum of outlets, from sketches to short stories in newspapers and magazines, and from the popular essay to the narrative poem. Through an understanding of the people in the stalls and the circle, we may look deeper into what is arguably a period of quiet revolution in English letters.

George in many ways bestrode that dual highway, the parallel routes of popular song, placed in music hall and in the parlour, the concert and the very Victorian affair of the soirée.

1

A House of Entertainment

'From quiet homes and first beginning
Out to the undiscovered ends,
There's nothing worth the wear of winning
But laughter and the love of friends.'
Hilaire Belloc: *Dedicatory Ode*

George was born on 9 December 1847 into a world we in 2013 would know well – one dominated temporarily by financial panic. Two months before he was delivered into the world of London, there had been, as *The Daily News* reported, 'Panic in the City' and the editorial demanded that the government take a bold step and save everyone from the 'consequences of national insolvency.' Fortunately, the crash was avoided. Events closer to the culture George would know included the first appearance of Jenny Lind, which was at the Haymarket, and the death of Felix Mendelssohn at only 39, just a month before young George was born.

His first notable memory was watching the funeral of the Duke of Wellington, and he wrote that 'The crowd, the soldiers, and the magnificent funeral car' were 'still strongly engraven' on his memory when he sat down to write his autobiography, *A Society Clown*, published in 1888. His memory held plenty of information regarding his education, as he was from a family in which learning and culture were central to life. He recalled going to a school run by a Miss Adams, and later to a school in Haverstock Hill, a place called Massingham House, advertised in 1862 as 'a long-established school in which young gentlemen from the age of five to 12 are prepared for the public schools and colleges.' The fees were six guineas per quarter at that time, including laundry.

George started his schooling there in 1855 as a boarder, and his most vivid memory was being skilled at fooling, noting that Miss Eliza Hay (one of the sisters who ran the school) said that 'He gets on very well with his music, but I am afraid he will one day be a clown.' He learned piano from the other sister, Isabelle, and wrote that he became one of her favourite pupils.[10]

His grandfather, William, had married Lucy Briant of Whitchurch in Oxfordshire, and the household was in the grip of Thespis, there being an abundant theatrical talent in the ranks. George the First's brothers, William and Benjamin, had outstanding acting ability, and the former was indeed destined to be billed as 'The Young Roscius' (named after the famous Roman actor of the first century AD, Quintus Gallus Roscius, whose name had become synonymous with great acting). This was after they settled in Reading. There, young William made his stage debut in London in 1824 at the Coburg Theatre, and Benjamin did successful comedy acts on tour, from the early 1803, then later became a maker of artificial limbs, based in Fleet Street.

George the First married and settled in Reading, and there he started what was to be a life on the road, appearing wherever he could obtain a booking. With the acting pedigree of his brothers, the stage as a profession was in the genes, and it is clear that his life as an entertainer appealed to his son from an early age, as George was to present family entertainments, emulating his father, from being very young.

In the 1850s, young George shifted with the family to an address very near his school in Haverstock Hill, number 36, called Manor Lodge. Soon after, he moved up to the North London Collegiate School, where he wore a mortar-board and became friends with E H Dickens, a nephew of the novelist. In the 1840s the press had campaigned for the clergy to be more involved with education, and a decade before that some schools had formed unions with King's College. Canon Thomas Dale at St Pancras became the driving force behind the London Collegiate School for Boys, which had followed on from the famous school with that name for girls, an institution springing from Frances Buss' school of 1845 in Kentish Town. Dale's school opened in 1850, with his curate, E H Williams, as the Head. On offer was either a commercial or a classical education, for nine guineas a year. Dale was appointed to the Board of Control in 1850 and examined candidates for admission into the East India College. [11]

Dale was very involved in crusades for the improvement of the workers, and with the fight against poverty and deprivation. In 1846 he had addressed the Society for the Improvement of the Labouring Classes at their annual meeting, when he was residentiary of St Paul's, where he 'bore testimony to the disorders occasioned by bad drainage, ineffective ventilation and narrow domiciles.' In his farewell address at St Mary's, Regent's Park, in 1858 he 'called on those present to a practical proof of their love of Christ by contributing to the schools.'

George developed interests in music, riding a bicycle, and in music. In an age when the bare-knuckle fighters walked around the streets as popular but familiar celebrities, he somehow managed to arrange a visit to the house of the great boxer, Ben Caunt, a heavyweight who would, when George met him, have been retired from the ring, working as a labourer. Caunt's last fight was in 1857 with Nat Langham, to whom young George was introduced by Caunt, who was later to become the landlord of the Coach and Horses in St Martin's Lane in his last years. George was in contact with these men at a momentous time in the history of boxing: Caunt and Langham had fought for 60 rounds and the match had been declared a draw. George had been excited by the 'pugilistic fever' across the land in the 1850s and had met two giants of the sport – without his parents' knowledge.[12]

As for cycling, it is in that hobby that we have a telling glimpse of George the First and his family life. George wrote that his father joined in with the cycling, calling him one of 'we three boys', and noting that 'I often think many fathers would find it to their advantage if they followed his example.' We have a strong image of his father when we read that he was 'only a little over five feet and much inclined to embonpoint.'

George the First was born on 20 August 1821, and rather than follow his two elder brothers onto the stage, he trained as a journalist, learning his craft at first with the *Reading Mercury*, but then moving to London, as most ambitious literary men did (and perhaps still do); speculation must assert that he saved cash, because he managed to obtain rooms in The Temple, and then found work with *The Times*. Whatever he did in his first assignments with that great paper, it was as a crime reporter that he impressed, working at Bow Street, the busy central police court in Covent Garden which had been the site of the famous magistracy of the Fielding brothers in the mid-eighteenth century – Henry the novelist and John, the blind magistrate who perhaps did most to raise the profile of that often reviled public office.

George the First was also a lecturer, and the histrionic bent was arguably as strong in him as in his brothers, but it expressed itself more in the arena of education and popular literature than in dramatic performance in such venues as music halls or in supportive roles in the theatre itself. His work at *The Times*, sitting with notebook in the

Bow Street court, was clearly so good that it became the basis for his financial security, allowing him to use a stand-in whenever he wanted to go on provincial tour with his readings and lectures.

He became immensely successful and popular on the circuit of the 'institutions' – various adult education establishments which had burgeoned after the first Mechanics Institutes in 1823. When he first started this work in the 1850s, as George was going to school in St Pancras, readings and lectures in adult education and entertainment were booming. Not only were there various clubs and societies for working people, but there was also the Penny Reading movement. This had started in the late 1850s, one claimant to the creation of these being Charles Sulley, editor of the *Ipswich Express*. But the origins are unclear. One writer in 1865 noted that 'In another part of the country, at Hanley in the Potteries, a similar movement had already been commenced, instigated, we believe, by Mr Samuel Taylor ... with a view to provide innocent amusement for the working classes ...'[13]

According to Samuel Taylor, the movement began in this way:

'At first the admission was free, the funds being supplied
by a few friends to popular movement. But one evening
a working man from the body of the hall arose, and
voluntarily proposed that an admission fee of one penny
should be charged in future. This proposition was
received with acclamation...'[14]

George the First realised that there were multiple opportunities for a literary man with a gift for expressing humour, with audiences ranging from working-class enthusiasts to such events as soirees and entertainments for the leisured class. Various researchers into public readings and all varieties of reading aloud in mid-Victorian Britain have shown why this flowering occurred at the time. Alison Byerley has looked at the influences on the public reading and lecturing culture, and she found that the theatricality of such reading was linked to a number of elements, ranging from elocution manuals to one-man shows. Lecturing and reading to audiences was also, of course, enhanced and popularised by Charles Dickens, and before him, Charles Mathews, as Byerley explains:

'Charles Mathews was one of the first successful
solo performers and exerted considerable influence on

Dickens, who saw him perform many times. Mathews was an actor who achieved considerable success in a wide variety of character roles and gradually developed a one-man programme ... His first shows were lectures of a sort, narratives in which he would recount a journey and act out the parts of various people along the way.'[15]

He gave his first professional lecture at the Reading mechanics institution on 21 December 1847, and it was a great success; the report in the *Reading Mercury* commented: 'The address embraced an allusion to the history of wit and witty authors ... it was an evening's entertainment of a most amusing character'. The review goes on to give us an impression of the man as he performed: 'But Mr Grossmith's voice must be heard, and his gestures seen, to properly estimate his comic powers. A wit himself, a practiced and accomplished reciter, an exquisite mimic, with an admirable perception of the grotesque and the ludicrous ...'[16]

He had made links with the Reading institution, which had been established around 1825, meeting in rented rooms in Bear Yard, Bridge Street; it then moved to 55 St Mary's Butts and began offering lectures on the principal sciences, providing a library, and had a paid librarian. After financial problems, it reopened in 1840, when George the First became aware of the possibilities it offered, and after acquiring more funds and support, it named itself, in 1843, the Reading Literary, Scientific and Mechanics' Institution, and moved into premises at London Street.

Reading in the early nineteenth century, as W M Childs (writing in 1910) explained, was a place with educational and cultural aspirations beyond the norm. Childs lists a Book Club founded in 1802, the Permanent Library and Literary Institution, appearing in 1807-8 and then the Philosophical Institution of 1831. As well as the Mechanics' Institution there was the Athenaeum, 'open to all classes, creeds and parties, and the decision taken at a public meeting in December, 1841' to form the organisation.[17] All this was in a very encouraging intellectual climate for the arts generally in Reading. As Childs adds: 'The zeal for popular education, the development of the *Reading Mercury* between 1820 and 1830 from a lifeless catalogue of news into a spirited organ of political opinion, the restless curiosity aroused by the new scientific achievements and inventions, the prolonged and passionate advocacy of political reforms are all indicative … of intellectual life and the movement of ideas.'[18]

At the same time, at the height of Regency cultural improvement and the cultivation of the arts, theatre in Reading flourished, and both brothers of George the First found openings for their talents, in a context of a new, liberated attitude:

> 'It was remarked in 1810 that partly "owing to the bigotry of the Methodists and partly to " the immoderate thirst for gain that pervades every class of shopkeepers, dramatic performances in this town are not only treated with neglect and received with disgust, but the people are instructed from the pulpit to consider them as dangerous to religion"… and a generation later observations similar in tone were repeated' but 'In 1815 a comedy by Talfourd was performed … in 1827 a tragedy by Miss Mitford and in 1840 Talfourd's Glencoe. In 1826, and for some years subsequently, much interest was taken in the performances of Masters B and W H Grossmith, natives of the town …'[19]

The Grossmith family were having a notable impact on Reading society, and there is more than a hint of pride in the last sentence above, written by a local historian who grew up in the area in the 1860s when the Grossmiths were very much in the press and talked about in society.

The notion of attending lectures and being informed, in a world in which knowledge was patently a source of power and success, was one part of a lust for learning at this time. One survey of London education explains the context very precisely: '… each appealed to different classes of the public, so that lecturers were obliged to grade their material to the right level for their audience, and lecturing was rightly looked upon as a fine art. The scarcely literate adults who had been denied opportunity and who needed the utmost encouragement and sympathy in their efforts to expand their minds deserved the very best instruction …' [20] George the First's choice of literature was made at a time when English literature and classics were arriving on the scene as part of a necessary liberal education. Just a little before the lecturing began, the University of London had been created, with the inclusion of a Chair of English Literature. The idea of reading from and explaining 'the English humorists' as George the First did, was partly an extension of the typical subjects of essays and *belles lettres* in the highbrow reviews of the time, but partly also a nod of approval to the place of comedy and wit in mainstream English writing.

When the family moved to London, he was continuing this work alongside the crime reporting. He had succeeded with lectures on writers, and continued this. One venue he found welcoming was the Whittington Club, created at the Crown and Anchor, Arundel Street, the Strand, by the writer Douglas Jerrold in 1846. This was established as a cheap club for men and women of the middle- and upper-middle classes 'with a view to throw open to them those increased physical comforts and facilities for moral and intellectual education which are the most attractive characteristics of modern London life, but which, in the absence of individual wealth, associated members alone can command.'[21] It offered classes in chemistry, modern languages, music, and dancing, for an annual subscription of a guinea. The Crown and Anchor burnt down in 1854 but the Whittington Club carried on until 1873. In 1850, George the First was advertised as offering a lecture there on 'The Writings of Charles Dickens.' Two years earlier, fresh from Reading, he had repeated his lecture on wit and humour in literature there also. A similar place was the British and Foreign Institute, formed in 1843 and providing 'weekly soirees or literary conversazione and … courses of popular lectures on subjects of general interest, with the constant use of a library for reference.'[22]

George the First is reputed, according to Tony Joseph, to have been the model for Mr Pickwick, and has been accounted a close friend of Dickens, but strangely, the most recent biographies of Dickens, by Michael Slater and by Claire Tomalin, make no reference to this. Physically, he certainly had the shape and rotundity of Pickwick, but as that novel was published in 1837 (after serial publication the previous year), when George the First was only 16, it seems unlikely.

We have a photo of him, used in his son Weedon's book, *From Studio to Stage*, showing him in a relaxed posture, a man of whom Weedon wrote, 'He could keep an audience thoroughly entertained for a couple of hours without any music or costume to assist him, and he never used notes.'[23]

The family atmosphere created by George the First and his wife, Louisa Weedon Briant, was wonderful for a child. In their early days in London, before success escalated, there was an atmosphere of fun and plenty of social events. But George the First was away on the road, earning a good income from his lectures and readings in the provinces. He was busy from Nottingham to Worcester, writing to make appointments and explain what subjects he could offer, being his own secretary, manager and reference librarian – a one-man show with a range of literature and jokes in his repertoire, ready for all audiences in his chosen venues, from self-improving workers to middle-class leisured types with a lust for culture and the arts. In 1863 he was at the Newark Mechanics' Institute, which was a typical success story of that movement, having started in 1836, and by 1874 having built a membership of almost 450 men. A year later, he gave two lectures at the Shrewsbury Institute, giving the first lecture of the winter course on 10 October, and three days later speaking on 'A Sketch of the Life and Character of the Modern Humorists.' We may gather something of the nature of the event when we note that he spoke 'in the music hall.'

The Penny Reading entertainment started in the late 1850s, the name being adopted after an audience member had suggested a penny charge instead of free entry. As the events became more popular, there was a problem with what today we might call quality control: the fact was that such work was open to those who were rather more in the category of poseurs and mountebanks than genuine speakers with a proper knowledge of their subject or a flair for the delivery of interesting and entertaining material. As one commentator wrote:

> 'But lecturing, like many other good things, has been
> abused. It was at an early date – droll idea! – supposed
> to be a remunerative speculation. Awful was the rush
> of needy, greedy, hungry adventurers (male and female)
> who resorted to it for a livelihood! Everybody, whether
> qualified or not, set up in business for himself as a
> lecturer, puffed himself into a quasi-notoriety and became
> at once a self-appointed professional.'[24]

Few memoirs of this period dealing with the various public readings and touring performers add insights into the acts and the locations, but in William Morton's account of being involved in the amateur theatre business we have valuable comments. Morton was a journalist-turned-theatre-manager, at first with the Greenwich Theatre in London, and then in Hull. In his early days he worked in Southport, and he has left an account of George the First. In Southport 'The only building in which entertainment could be held was the Town Hall with a seating capacity of 500 … I organised a series of concerts and other entertainments and introduced many of the famous people of the scientific and musical world, also a well-known humorist Mr George Grossmith (father and grandfather of the famous actors of that name … I think I booked three engagements with this fascinating personage. His programme was always of a highly humorous description. He was really a comedian in evening dress. He never failed to send his audience home delighted.'[25] Morton then describes George the First's 'platform':

'Before his first visit I wrote asking what preparations he desired on the platform. "A small four-legged table with a cover to reach the floor." I could not guess why the cover was to reach the floor, so when he came I put the questions: "Are you going to do conjuring tricks?" His answer was, "Well, my dear Sir, if the people were to get a sight of my legs they would hurry for the exits."'[26]

George the First certainly made his mark. Morton adds that 'I may forget many other professional entertainers but never my friend, little pleasant "podgy" George Grossmith.'[27]

George the First was rising to success and to the status of a minor celebrity at a time when popular entertainment was responding to the new audiences, generated by the rise of the urban populations across the land, in the aftermath of the first great Industrial Revolution. George comments in his memoir that 'For eight or nine months of the year we did not see much of the master of the house, for he was away lecturing; but we always welcomed his return home, generally on Saturdays. In the summer we had more leisure; he was brimful of humour, and there were few people so good at repartee.'[28]

Manor Lodge was a house of fun. We know from George's memoir what kind of play and theatre went on within the walls. He provides a full programme, explaining what a 'party' at home in his childhood was like. There was good conversation, dancing and singing, and 'Banquet of the Elders in the Culinary Caverns of the Regions Below.' It was for one of these parties that George the First wrote a burlesque of *Hamlet* which George loved so much that he 'afterwards did it at the residences of Mr Toole and John Hollingshead to "grown-up" parties.'[29] This was a twenty-minute piece in which a spoof of the play was given, particularly relishing the bizarre comedy of the last multiple death scene, in which the 'dead' characters start to talk about themselves, with lines in which they all argue as to who will speak the tag for the scene.

George's brother, Weedon, gives another insight into the family life and its tendency to encourage rather wild activity. For instance, he recalled the time when he and George experimented with dangerous substances. They decided to 'make gas from turpentine or benzolin ...' and the results were alarming: 'Needless to say, in making the gas, it shot up from the narrow neck of the can with a hissing, roaring noise, and with as much power, I should think as would propel an engine.'[30]

George recalled that his home was also a place where celebrities gathered, such was the widening social sphere his father moved in. After all, we need to note here that George the First had moved in social spheres totally in contrast from institutes and music halls: he was one of the founders of the Savage Club, for instance. This was founded in 1857, and the first annual general meeting was held the next year. Andrew Halliday, later a friend of George's, was the first chronicler, and it is clear that George the First had made some powerful and influential friends in literary and journalistic society. The Savage Club members first met at the Crown Tavern in Drury Lane, but then moved in 1863 to Gordon's Hotel, Covent Garden, and later to several other locations.

We can understand exactly what the atmosphere was like at the Savage Club at the time, from memoirs, such as this account of a typical evening there, written by Marshall P Wilder:

> 'Saturday night at the Savage is a gala day. Maybe a night may not seem a day but it lasts nearly as long- at the Savage. It begins with a dinner at five O'clock; after an hour or so of eating and drinking the tables are cleared, the incense of burning tobacco begins to perfume the air, and the chairman, who was appointed by his predecessor for one week only calls on some member to do something. The member must respond; apologies are never accepted. A man may sing a song, tell a story, speak a piece or make faces.'[31]

As Wilder sums it up: 'There is no more formality there than at a Methodist camp meeting.'[32]

An important element in this socialising and career success for George the First was his freemasonry. It is no accident that in 1887 the Savage Club was proposed as a new Masonic lodge. When George the First and George teamed up to work together on the stage, their debut was at the Masonic lodge in Birmingham. There were strong connections between the theatrical profession and freemasonry at this time. Augustus Harris, manager of the Drury Lane theatre, was a freemason, and as Andrew Prescott has researched, 'Harris conceived the idea of forming a lodge which would meet in a specially furnished Masonic temple within the Drury lane theatre itself.'[33] As Prescott points out, we need to grasp the nature of freemasonry in the mid- to late-nineteenth century to understand how it impacted on the artistic and theatrical community. The movement was on a massive scale at the time: 'The growing social prestige of freemasonry in the second half of the nineteenth century was expressed in many ways. The imposing headquarters of English freemasonry at Freemason's Hall in Great Queen Street in London was rebuilt and extended in 1864, and lodges in provincial cities also built opulent Masonic halls.'[34] Prescott also notes that there were 382 lodges in London by 1894, compared with 100 fifty years before.[35]

Being a freemason at that time clearly accelerated access to the higher echelons of one's chosen career. George the First had the required social ease and conversational ability to make himself welcome in such circles; he was decidedly a man with great bonhomie and a cultured manner. He made friends easily, and drew them into his social circle. He was far from being one of those touring lecturers who simply peddled their one special patch of expertise around the clubs and societies; he had presence and he generated fun and pleasure, both in the family and beyond, into his widening social circle, as he settled into London life. George would benefit immensely from his father's personality.

George wrote that such famous people as Henry Irving, Kate and Ellen Terry, Charles Wyndham and the painter Luke Fildes, were among the guests at Haverstock Hill. He notes that 'the brothers Brough' came too – they were founding members of the Savage Club; William Brough wrote some of the dramatic material for the German Reeds, who were to employ George early in his career as a pianist entertainer, and Robert Brough was a writer too.

Writers and artists at this time mixed in a number of clubs; it was essential to be seen and known, and London never slept. George

Augustus Sala, a journalist writing in 1858, described London 'twice round the clock' – explaining the hunger for socialising and entertainment at all hours of the day and night. Sala explained the vast spectrum of clubs available, listing eighteen of them, adding that 'Clubbism is a great mystery, and its adepts must be cautious how they explain its shibboleth to the outer barbarians. Men have been expelled from clubs ere now for talking or writing about another members' whiskers.'[36]

But George the First's travel across the land on the new railways involved finding a deputy for the Bow Street crime reporting, and George and his brother Weedon left the Collegiate School just at the right time to help in the family enterprise. Weedon, future collaborator on *The Diary of a Nobody*, went to the West London School of Art, and George had the intention of reading for the Bar. That legal aspiration was possible without an Oxbridge education, and could be attained by what today we might call 'work-based study.' But the problem with that was financial. He needed to earn, and Bow Street opened up, as his father was able to do the requisite wheeling and dealing to have son George fill in with the pen, sit in the court room, and learn the crime reporter's trade.

The notion of reading for the Bar was what a young man did at the time if other professions closed or appeared to be unthinkable. George was growing into young adulthood in many ways a typical middle-class son of the period: he had an interest in bicycles and in photography; he dabbled in music and drama; he went to a good school and had a commercial rather than classical education; he made friends – influential ones as well – and he was in the hands of a father who knew the benefits of acquiring what we might now call 'transferable skills.' He had learned the piano and also learned shorthand: his father made sure of that. But reading for the Bar was always a last option. Even literary men who had a university education saw the law as a rather perfunctory move; Max Pemberton, who graduated from Cambridge in the 1880s, wrote, 'I got a degree in law –heaven knows why – and was duly patted on the head by the Vice Chancellor and styled Most Learned.'[37] Pemberton, like George, became a journalist and writer, with a penchant for the stage.

2

THE WRITER AT BOW STREET

'He do the police in different voices'
T S Eliot: original title for *The Waste Land*

So it was that George was equipped to work *pro tem* at Bow Street. He had the shorthand and he had his father as mentor. That in itself must have been a major challenge. Charles Dickens, doing a similar reporting job at the Doctor's Commons thirty years earlier, wrote about learning shorthand, and he explained the difficulty, helping the modern reader to understand just what was required:

> 'The changes that were rung upon dots, which in such a position meant such a thing, and in such another position something else, entirely different; the wonderful vagaries that were played by circles; the unaccountable consequences that resulted from marks like flies' legs; the tremendous effects of a curve in the wrong place, not only troubled my waking hours, but reappeared before me in my sleep.'[38]

But of course, father was away entertaining at the institutes. Tony Joseph has pointed out just how difficult the actual physical demands of writing the reports was; he points out that twelve copies of each report had to be made, with the use of a stylus rather than a pen or pencil: 'The amount of pressure required to produce twelve clear copies ... not to mention the state of the hands after sweating at this for any length of time ... could well be imagined.'[39] What was Bow Street like at that time? The court George came to know had been built in 1825 on the site of the previous court which had been established by the Fielding brothers, close to Covent Garden. Just around the corner, Dr Johnson had first met Boswell at Tom Davies' bookshop, and those two writers would have relished people-watching, sitting there at the bookshop window in the midst of the lower orders and the criminal classes. It was indeed the focus of criminal law in the city, being the magistrate court at which all crime from within the heart of London was first heard, from petty theft to murder and major fraud.

It was a 'police court' – also referred to in reports as a 'police office' – and it was a workful, constantly busy place, with a tide of criminal and officers ebbing and flowing day and night. George had plenty of time to kill in his time at the court, and he saw and knew both the office and the court itself. We know what it was like from Dickens' novel *Oliver Twist* and, in a more direct documentary fashion, from his piece called 'The Metropolitan Protectives'. Dickens describes the office:

'In the right-hand corner of this room –which is a bare room like a guard-house without the drums and muskets – is a dock, or a space railed off for prisoners: opposite, a window breast-high at which an Inspector always presides day and night to hear charges. Passing by a corner door into his office … we find it much like any other office – inky, dull and quiet…'[40]

Dickens could also convey the more emotional side of the Bow Street hearings, as when he describes young Oliver Twist's appearance there: 'The office was a front parlour, with a panelled wall. Mr Fang sat behind a bar, at the upper end; and on one side of the door was a sort of wooden pen in which poor little Oliver was already deposited: trembling very much at the awfulness of the scene.'[41]

Montagu Williams, a barrister who also worked as an actor, also worked in Bow Street at the time. Justice Flowers and Justice Henry, whom George knew well, were well known to Williams:

'The magistrates at Bow Street were Sir Thomas Henry, Mr Vaughan and Mr Flowers; and in reference to the last-named, who was familiarly known as "Jimmy" Flowers, I may mention that he was an old Temple pupil of my Father's, and one of the most kind-hearted creatures that ever lived … Sir Thomas Henry, as chief magistrate, only sat in court about two days a week For he had to transact all the Home Office business, and hear the Extradition cases…'[42]

Bow Street was also a draw for the crowd, lusting for some excitement rather more interesting that what was on stage. George Augustus Sala explains that the people out on the town and the idle underclass enjoyed the sight of the police van outside the court being loaded:

'When the hour of departure arrives, you see the pavement and carriageway of Bow Street studded with a choice assemblage of the raggedry, ruffianry, felonry, misery, drunkardry and drabbery, whom the infamous hundred of Drury, and the scarcely less infamous tithing of Covent, have cast out into a thoroughfare which, two hours hence, will be re-echoing to the wheels of carriages bearing noble lords and ladies to listen to the delicious Bosio (alas!) in the Traviata or the enchanting notes of Tamberlik in Otello.'[43]

George had some guidance in the new job. He wrote in his memoir that his father already had an assistant in the work: 'I received instructions from my father, who was just starting for Liverpool, that as Mr Courtenay was ill, I must go and "do" Bow Street. Mr Courtenay used to do all the reporting at Bow Street Police Court during my father's absence on his lecture tours.' Not much is known about John Kelley Courtenay; he was born c1830 in Chelsea and lived in St Pancras at Frederick Place at first, and was living in Covent Garden at the time of the crime reporting. We know that he married Mary Faulkner in Kent in 1857. His father, James, had also been a reporter, and his son Austin also followed that career. John Kelly Courtenay died while George was engaged in the Bow Street work, in 1869, so George was left as sole assistant to his father when some major cases in British criminal history came before him at the court. There were small matters such as assaults in street arguments, thefts and robberies. But in the late 1860s there was first of all the last phase of what was known as the 'garotting' panic, the Fenian bombings at Clerkenwell, and the infamous turf fraud involving City of London detectives. George saw the first hearings of these, having to cope with far more than shorthand and clear English: he also had to learn a great deal about the criminal justice process and the workings of the law.

George saw Fenian assassins who were destined to be hanged after trial in a higher court. A bill to suspend Habeas Corpus was passed in

February 1866 and the Lord Lieutenant was given special powers of arrest. It was controversial in the extreme: John Bright criticised it as 'a blot upon the reign of the Queen'. The most notable result of this was that Americans in Ireland who had been building alliances with republicans, went home. The focus of activities was going to be across the ocean and that would have important consequences for the new detectives. The Habeas Corpus principle was one of preventing arrests on suspicion and also of making it illegal for a person to languish in gaol for indefinite periods. It also dictates that every person has a right to trial by jury. In other words, the suspension was an act familiar to Britons today – it was a response to terrorism.

There was a history of Fenian bombing and the Special Irish Branch was well-briefed on that. Williamson had been active during the first real campaigns of 1867, a period of desperation and extremism on the part of the Fenians. In 1866 a force of Fenians had tried to invade Canada after capturing Fort Erie. In 1867 they had attempted to attack Chester Castle and in 1867 they at last had a terrible impact on English life. Although a rising led by James Stephens failed in Ireland, the war was carried into England. On 8 September 1867 a police officer, Sergeant Brett, was murdered in Manchester while guarding two Fenian prisoners, Kelly and Deasy, and the killers were executed, thus providing the Fenian movement with some martyrs and they became known as 'The Manchester Martyrs.'

On 13 December that year came the Clerkenwell explosion. Twelve people died and sixty yards of prison wall were ruined. Over a hundred people were wounded. If nothing else, these events had the effect of making English people aware of the issues in Irish society. Between these first major terrorist activities and the new scares of the 1880s, Gladstone fought for reform on the Irish questions of Home Rule and changes in the established church. But even during the 1880s, during the new bombing campaign, the Home Rule bill was defeated.

In contrast, George wrote up accounts of humour and human foibles, including the fascinating saga of the men in female attire. This became known as the Female Impersonation Case (April 1870). Ernest Boulton and Frederick Park were charged with intent to commit an offence at the Strand Theatre. Police officers had trailed them and kept them under surveillance for some time, checking out their Wakefield Street pad where they found a large number of items of female dress. Technically, they were charged with 'conspiring and inciting persons to commit an unnatural offence.' In the end, transvestitism was not decided to be a crime, and efforts to try to ascertain that sodomy was taking place failed.

George witnessed a huge crowd for the trial and the subject had both notoriety and topicality. At this time, the acrobat, Farini, was dressed as a woman – Mademoiselle Lulu – and performing as 'the female gymnast' while singing a refrain called *Wait Til I'm a Man* in his act at the Holborn Amphitheatre. 'She' had received a flood of love letters from admirers.

In court, as George scribbled down the facts, they wore their female clothing. They were not given bail, and so the mob were entertained by the sight of the two being hurried into a Black Maria on their way to gaol. George Augustus Sala's account of London life at the time shows and describes the process from court to van and gaol, showing exactly what George would have witnessed.

The case had a huge social impact, and in fact the two men were fictionalised in a later novel, *The Sins of the Cities of the Plain*, and they were also featured in a play by Martin Lewton, *Lord Arthur's Bed*, in 2008. Of course, there is the wonderful irony that just a few years later, the child star Vesta Tilley made cross-dressing vice versa immensely popular on the stage.

George's reports convey the drama with great versatility and life. At one point, a letter from Louis Hurt written to Boulton was read aloud, and the resulting dialogue could have been material for a later Grossmith act. This is how the young reporter conveyed the scene, starting with a part of the letter:

'Let me ask your advice. A young lady whose family are friends of mine is coming down. She is a charmingly dressed beautiful fool ... I can marry her. You know I could never care for her, but is the bait tempting enough for me to make this further sacrifice to respectability? People don't mind what one does on £30,000 a year ... What shall I do?' 'Mr Besley said, on looking at this letter, that it was in a woman's handwriting. Mr Poland said he saw no resemblance ...Mr Poland explained the term 'drag' was used in one of the letters in connexion with a trip to the derby, and everyone knew what that meant. Mr Flowers thought it a pity that the letters could not have been read privately. An argument then followed upon the question of the magistrate's discretionary power to take bail, and it was urged that prosecution would take the form of a charge of conspiracy with intent etc ...'[44]

George ends the report with this comment: 'The court was densely crowded throughout the enquiry by a class of persons very superior to the ordinary visitors to be seen at Bow Street.'[45] In other words, this was a spectacle to rival anything seen on a stage at one of the many theatres of the time which offered burlesques and satires on men and manners – in fact, just the kind of material that George Grossmith was to relish. In his seat at the court, he was enjoying the process of transmuting reality into something rich and strange – and highly entertaining.

George was in the habit of giving in to a certain level of boredom at times, and would wander off for a while, or take a very long lunch. This entailed missing part of a very high-profile case, and one that every journalist would long to happen, was the arrest of a young man called Arthur O'Connor in 1872 – O'Connor being one of Queen Victoria's would-be assassins. George wrote in his memoir, 'On one occasion I returned and found Mr John Brown giving evidence in a charge against a lad for at attempt upon the life of our Most Gracious Majesty. However, I have managed to write a case just as well when I have not been present as when I have.'[46]

What he partly missed was a major commotion. It had all started at ten in the morning, so perhaps George did not arrive until late that afternoon or he would have known the magnitude of the case, and the would-be assassin was not in the dock until two that afternoon. A huge crowd gathered outside, and later, His Royal Highness Prince Leopold arrived at court. He was joined by other aristocrats and top brass, including Lord Charles Fitzroy, General Hardinge and Colonel Henderson. The man George saw giving testimony was actually the man who had saved the Queen, as he had grabbed O'Connor as he raised a pistol and pointed it towards Victoria, who had Leopold with her, and who had moved sideways, shouting, 'Save me!' [47]

The account of his Bow Street work implies that at times he struggled to commit himself full-time to the work. Between 1866 and 1869, George was taught and guided by John Courtenay: George wrote that Courtenay helped him to edit and revise the reports, and George learned a lot about writing from his new friend. In fact the older man also helped with George's creative writing. George was, it is clear, feverishly trying to make it as a writer. He admits in his memoir that he tried to write various varieties of prose and even chapters of novels and says that Courtenay helped him with 'little occasional articles or verses which I wrote for humorous periodicals' and Courtenay also wrote short pieces which were part of amateur theatricals George was beginning to do.[48]

Clearly, he was at that stage in a writer's development at which explorations and trials of genre, style and the natural narrative voice tend to point the way towards success through sheer practice. He also ventured into self-publishing, another learning experience of many writers, including Bernard Shaw, who published his own novels before attaining success as a playwright. George's book was a publication with contributions from himself and some friends. He describes it in his memoir:

> 'I spent part of the spare time, in my earlier days at Bow Street, in editing a paper called Ourselves at Home. It was published by a printer for me, and consisted of eight pages … with very little matter – much spacing and very big type. The cost was ten shillings a week for which we had fifty or a hundred copies … The periodical terminated after thirteen numbers, because our friends could not be induced to read it, much less buy it. It died a natural death on March 8th 1867.'[49]

In fact, George was burgeoning into taking his first steps in the world of popular entertainment. What is not explicit in the outline of events in George's life at this time is just how much he was working hard to make his way in writing of any kind. We know that he was learning by doing; trying his hand at anything as he followed up an idea. In that, he is entirely typical of the novice writer with several collections of chapters kept in desk drawers, one day to be completed. But on top of that, it is highly likely that he was sharp and receptive, with an eye to potential openings for his creative spirit. Gradually, a number of opportunities opened up, and through his father's contacts, largely one assumes in his Masonic circles, both father and son began to benefit. George the First is a template of the kind of performer who maximised his talent, moving laterally into new contexts all the time. George followed him in that.

After all, by the late 1860s, when George was in his early twenties, he had a lot to offer – in modern terms, a wide portfolio if it came to an interview or an application. He was qualified as a reporter and journalist, he could act and he could sing and play the piano. His talent at that early stage could have been pointed towards any one of a number of outlets from music hall to informal event and from readings to regular classical or revue contexts. That versatility was soon to find a number of scenarios, offering, as with his father, complementary activity and income, to add to the work for *The Times*.

One huge asset George had was the piano: by the middle years of the century, the upright piano had become affordable to middle-class families, and the popularity of the instrument for 'at homes' and for basic musical education within the family was booming when George first set about entertaining people at his piano. The Broadwood company, by the 1860s, was selling uprights at any sum between 80 down to 45 guineas, and, as Judith Flanders has explained, by 1850, 'about 83,000 families had an annual income of between £150 and £400.'[50] There was, indeed, a piano mania in Britain in the two decades after 1860. Where there is an amateur passion for music, there will be a growing and enthusiastic audience for professional musical performance. In George's case, his skill in music, combined with the satirical song and mimicry of social types, made the perfect and topical recipe for success as a comic performer.

If we add to these background trends the fact that the Theatres Act of 1843 finally opened up venues other than theatres to be places where some types of drama could be performed, then there is a sense that all kinds of performance venues were opening up as George came through to become a professional entertainer. But he also discovered that there were opportunities for his music and comedy in other, more small-scale and intimate venues too: he was to learn to be an all-rounder, someone who could put on a show almost anywhere for almost anyone. Also, as he was to learn, agencies for musical performers were also beginning to expand and become more energetic in looking for talent, particularly from the late 1850s.

George provided plenty of explanation on his musical abilities. He said that he 'played a good deal by ear' and that he made up his own songs from an early age; he disarmingly described his voice as of 'penny whistle' quality and that he loved to entertain at every opportunity.[51] Then there is the question of influence, and with that in mind, the name of John Parry has to be mentioned. George the First took his son to the Gallery of Illustration to see Parry the piano entertainer and the result of this was, in George's words, that he 'infused not only a new life, but a totally different style into my work.'[52]

The Gallery of Illustration was an interesting venue. It was a theatre, but under the guise of being many other things too. It was in Regent Street, at first the home of the architect, John Nash; by George's time, it was best described as a centre of entertainment and the arts, run by Thomas German-Reed and his wife, Priscilla. Legally, they were not allowed to produce plays, but they found a way to present drama, by having short sketches and comic acts on their stage; they also had small-scale operas in their programmes. John Parry was one of their stars. His full name was John Orlando Parry, born in 1810, the son of a John Parry who was a Welsh musician of some fame in his homeland. His father taught him to sing and to play both piano and harp. Starting out as an entertainer in 1830, he was soon in demand at a number of places, and after spending some time in Italy, he returned to London and gradually won a reputation as a comic singer, appearing in music halls as well as at more formal venues, and in 1860 was recruited by the German-Reeds. George, watching this talented performer, would have learned the essentials of what was to become his own speciality – impersonations, gentle satire and songs with music. He died in 1879, having had a benefit concerts for him, including one at the prestigious Gaiety Theatre, in 1877.

George met several other characters who had an influence on his work at this time, as he was developing and beginning to see just how many opportunities there were for what he had to offer as entertainer and writer. He notes that people started asking him to parties, and his social circle inevitably widened; for instance, he met the writer and singer Henry S Leigh, known today perhaps as a comic poet, the author of one of the small comic masterpieces of English verse, *The Twins*. George said that, around 1870, Leigh was writing for *Fun* magazine, a publication akin to the famous *Punch* with satire and light-hearted social commentary being the main styles. George wrote, 'He was himself a great admirer of John Parry and when I became intimate with him, in after years, he used to show me how Parry sang 'Wanted, A Governess,' 'The Old Bachelor,' the 'Dejeuner a la Fourchette' etc., all of which I have sung myself at times.'[53]

He was also cutting his teeth at penny readings at this time; but a much more lucrative and significant advance in his career came with his events at the Royal Polytechnic Institution, also in Regent

Street not far from the Gallery. In 1878, Edward Walford gave this description of the Institution:

> '... founded in 1838 for the exhibition of novelties in
> the arts and in practical science ... the premises of this
> institution are capacious and well appointed and extend
> from the east entrance in Regent Street 320 feet in depth,
> including the mansion at no.5 Cavendish Square.' [54]

It was a very grand and ambitious establishment, offering, like the Whittington Club, classes in modern languages, Latin and science, and also courses of lectures on topical subjects. The guiding light of the place when George the First made contact was a charismatic character called Professor Henry Pepper, who wrote textbooks and gave scientific demonstrations, but who also had an eye for showmanship, display and sensation. He lectured there in 1847, but then became the Director in the early 1850s. A report in *The Morning Post* in 1861 as the Christmas season began, gives a vivid account of what the Polytechic offered:

> 'Under the skilful and spiritual management of Professor
> Pepper this excellent Institution is now conducted in
> a manner which gives it the strongest claims upon the
> patronage of the public. The whole of the galleries
> containing admirable mechanical and geological models,
> and a vast number of other interesting objects, are
> now thrown open to the visitors; popular novelties in
> science, arts and manufactures are continually brought
> forward; and in very department of the establishment the
> entertaining and the instructive are commingled in a most
> effective and felicitous combination.' [55]

On the entertainment side, under Pepper's direction and management, the Institution presented literary and dramatic readings, such as the Shakespeare readings by F D Cape in 1866, which was not much short of a full dramatic presentation, as one report described: 'The prettiest and most successful of the illusions conveyed is that of Ariel, who is represented floating through the air, only her head being visible, and in this position she sings the ever-captivating air, "Where the Bees Sucks ..."' [56]

Pepper was one of the most energetic and original movers and shakers in the world of the arts and popular science at the time. He was born in London in 1821, and after an education in science, he found this outlet for his abilities in the field of popular education, but went much further, surely earning the title of impresario and showman. Pepper's interest in experimenting with applications of electricity led him to arrange some sensational stunts and shows, such as the illumination of Trafalgar Square and St Paul's Cathedral at the time of the wedding celebrations of the Prince of Wales to Alexandra in 1863. His most culturally successful trick – in that it caused a flurry of interest in the press and in the streets – was his so-called 'ghost illusion.' This was a device originated by a man called Henry Dircks, and involved the projection of a human image onto the stage, apparently moving amongst 'living' actors; it was a trick done by the use of glass and light. So stunning was the effect, which Pepper had bought for reproduction from Dircks, that even Michael Faraday was lost for an explanation as to how it worked.

George started work with Pepper in 1870 and thought of himself, as always, as the 'clown' of the programmes. He began with a piece called *The Yellow Dwarf* which he describes in his memoir as 'exceedingly puerile' but it did well, and he followed that with something he really found to be his natural genre: *Human Oddities*. This was a forty-minute sketch, something made by himself and George the First, combining music, songs and impersonation.

Another big break allowing George to move from the Polytechnic into more directly theatrical contexts was an offer to tour with Mr and Mrs Howard Paul in late 1871. George doesn't say much about this in his memoir – simply that he was asked to join them on a seaside tour. He merely wrote, 'This was to me a delightful way of combining business with pleasure, and I particularly remember a delightful week at Scarborough.'[57]

The truth was that he had been paid a huge compliment by a couple who were a significant presence in the theatre of the time. Twelve years before this, they had appeared on the scene with a show called *Patchwork* at the Adelphi. In reviews, they were compared to the German-Reeds at the Gallery of Illustration, and it is clear that they depended on their pianist – at that time that post being filled by August Arnold – and like George, they delighted in stage caricature. *The Times* reviewer of *Patchwork* was impressed, particularly with 'Miss Featherstone' as Mrs Paul was known professionally before her marriage:

'Almost every one of her impersonations is illustrated
by a song, the music being always appropriate, and the
words delivered with no less humour than vivacity. Molly
Doolan, the Irish girl, with a ballad of "The Bowld Sojer
Boy" and Aurelia Gushinton, the sentimental unmarried
(and unmarriageable) lady, addicted to "moonlight and
Byron"… are both perfect in their way.'[58]

Their sketches were done in costume, and they were markedly
'at home with their audience.' Their need of what was called a 'musical
illustrator' was clear to reviewers who responded to their shows, so
George was ideal for them. Howard Paul was an American, and a
very talented all-round man of the theatre; he could write songs and
sketches as well as straight drama. His wife, Isabella Featherstone, was
equally talented and successful, having become known to the public
largely through her part of Captain Macheath in *The Beggar's Opera*,
and more recently, just a year before this tour, she had played Lady
Macbeth in a production at Drury Lane. She had started her acting
career in 1853 at The Strand, and then married Paul four years later;
in 1877 she was to work with George, playing Lady Sangazure in *The
Sorcerer*.

Howard Paul provides an example of the close-knit networking
the Grossmith theatrical circles provided for each other. Henry S Lee's
song and poem, *The Twins* just discussed, became a hit for Howard,
and he sang and performed the piece widely. A caricature of him
holding twins in his arms was made by the French cartoonist, Faustin
Betbeder. Paul was to be widowed in 1879 when Isabella died after
being taken ill while performing in Sheffield; she died in London at
the Pauls' home in Bedford Park. Howard took singer Letty Lind as
his partner for some time, and he became a very rich man, managing
the Alhambra Theatre in Leicester Square.[59]

Not only did George enjoy Scarborough itself, but he was a hit
with the local reporters, as these remarks about the Paul production
in *The Scarborough Gazette* show:

'Their last performance in Scarborough will take place
tomorrow when, in addition to a varied programme of
characters, Mrs Howard Paul will give her astounding
photograph of Mr Sims Reeves and sing "My Pretty Jane"
and "Love's Request." Mr Geo. Grossmith, jun., who has

appeared in conjunction with them, is an artiste of the John Parry school, and his Human Oddities, given with immense facial expression and admirable by-play, excited roars of laughter ...'60

Isabella was making the most of a gentle dig at Sims Reeves, who was an immensely popular tenor, singing in operas and concerts. As for George, it is clear from this review that he had mastered the art of patter – a complex mix of ad libs, anecdotes, clowning and some physical comedy, all with the piano mixing its sounds with George's light voice. He was being labelled a version of the great Parry, and in some ways his own art never went too far away from that of the master.

Shortly after the tour with the Pauls, George accelerated his career in terms of sheer effort and business: he finally teamed up with his father to present a show combining their talents. This was devised early in 1873, and then they organised a tour of various venues across the land. Interestingly, George married in the very midst of that string of tour dates. He had become engaged to Emmeline Rosa Noyce, a doctor's daughter. In George's memoir he wrote that they met at a party when she was 'a little maiden in a short frock and sash' and he wrote that 'We danced every dance together, but the fates decreed that we should not meet again for another three or four years.' Meet they did, and they married on 14 May 1873 at St Stephen's, Camden Town.

George had a very understanding new wife, because as they enjoyed a honeymoon jaunt, he took time out to do some work and earn money to finance their time together. The Pauls were in Liverpool, for instance, so he joined them while Rosa and he stayed with her relations nearby. On the surface, this looks like the lifestyle of a workaholic, but the fact is that George and Rosa needed the money. Rosa figures in an interview George did with *The Idler* in 1893. The photo shows her in a bamboo armchair, book in hand, wearing a floral-patterned dress with a high collar; her face conveys someone with a sense of humour, still perhaps a girl in her imagination, playful and good company. George would have needed someone like that. The interviewer was led into a 'special sanctum' into which nobody was allowed, except for Rosa. They were clearly very happy.

They were later to settle in Blandford Street, Dorset Square, which was, according to the author of *Old and New London* published around this time, once 'the site of what was in former times a noted cricket ground, and its present name is said to have been given to it 'after the great patron of cricket, the Duke of Dorset.'[61] It was well-placed for being close to any number of friends and clubs, just a short walk from Baker Street for instance, and adjoining locations which were popular for the social lives of theatre people and writers. One famous example is that of Conan Doyle, a lover – as George was – of clubs; he was one of the first members of the Crimes Club, which met in 1903 at the Great Central Hotel, close to Baker Street.

George the First came up with the idea that he and his son should tour together. It made perfect sense to combine George the First's personality as a speaker with George's music and humour. George was still working at Bow Street, but it was easy to find a locum, and the two Grossmiths were soon planning the repertoire and the structure of their show. Their first appearance at the Masonic Hall, Birmingham, was a trial of the material and of themselves as a duo. George very helpfully reproduced a programme from their tour together in *A Society Clown*. This was billed as 'a literary and musical entertainment.' There was no catchy, media-savvy title and no topical angle. It announced simple a union of two items and two talents. In Part One, George the First presented his 'gems from Charles Dickens' and George offered 'Seven Ages of Song' and a spoof of a penny reading, 'The Puddleton Penny Readings.' In Part Two, George the First did a Mark Twain anthology and George gave ' a new musical scena "In the Stalls."'[62]

Father and son were clearly very popular and there was no shortage of bookings. There is no doubt that the Masonic connections were proving very helpful in this success, but it needs to be stressed just how unusual what they offered was at that time. The combination of the literary and musical, with contrasting varieties of humour, would provide audiences already used to Dickensian readings with something extra, and the diversions of gentle satire and rather expressive rhetorical character projections would have offered the kind of mix flexible enough to appeal to all kinds of audience.

George's talent to amuse was finding openings in more and more places, and this was to continue in the years immediately after his marriage, with another possibility explained by a friend and fellow entertainer, Richard Corney Grain, known to posterity simply as Corney Grain. He too had worked at the Gallery of Illustration, and the two men were similar in their creative skills. In an interview,

Corney Grain told a story to illustrate this similarity: 'One of the most awkward incidents that occurred to me was when a gentleman said, "Do give us your sketch of the Drinking Fountain. I think it's quite your best." I said I would with pleasure but for the fact that I didn't know it, as it was Mr Grossmith's sketch.' [63]

Corney Grain was born in 1844, a farmer's son, but there were family connections with the legal profession, in that his cousin was the famous judge, Sir Travers Humphreys, and like George, Corney was at first intended for a life in the legal profession, and was called to the Bar in 1866, very much like his more famous confrère in the theatre, W S Gilbert. But in 1870 he, like George, met and worked with the German-Reeds, offering songs and sketches. When they met, Corney told George about the bookings available in society, at private parties. He took up the challenge, and his first appearances were encouraging. In fact, networking proved to be his forte once again, because in order to expand the opportunities for party bookings, he went to see George Dolby, the man who arranged readings for Dickens and was a close friend of the great novelist.

Dolby was confident that George would have plenty of party bookings. Dolby was a charismatic individual, and was arguably one of the principal movers and shakers in the world of popular entertainment outside the main theatrical world. In 1866, Dickens had contacted Chappell & Co, who were music publishers and concert promoters in New Bond Street, and a reading tour had been arranged, with Dolby as manager and arranger. Dolby had also worked with that other famous writer and lecturer of this time, Mark Twain, who had called Dolby a 'gladsome gorilla' – a reference to his large frame. Dolby had a cheery, outgoing personality and Dickens had taken to him, welcoming him as a close friend. Dolby was later to write a memoir of Dickens, so well did he know him.

This was the man who advised George, and who encouraged him to entertain at the parties of the wealthy social sets of London. Home entertainment was a lucrative and thriving market for anyone with musical gifts, and even more so for those who could make the guests laugh and take them away from their chats to actually listen to the songs and the music. Unfortunately that did not always happen, but the tendency for party people to treat the music on offer as merely a background sound led to a notable experience for George as he moved into this circle of business. He was singing for the guests at the home of the Duchess of St Albans in March 1875 when the experience of trying to sing and play in the midst of a horrendous noise of people's loud conversations and laughter overcame him.

His dilemma was observed by no less a person than Alexandra, Princess of Wales, who had married the future Edward VII twelve years earlier; she was very popular in high society, and very much a leader of fashion for the wealthy ladies. Alexandra walked to George and sat down to listen, plainly hinting that everyone else present should do likewise. This little sidelight in the middle of George's solo career is particularly interesting with regard to the Princess Alexandra. At that time, she had experienced her husband's serious illness in 1871, when he was not expected to pull through, and then there was the shame of the Prince's entanglements with various mistresses. The Alex who helped George, and who possibly gave him the boost he needed just at the right time, was described vividly by Hesketh Pearson who noted that she was: 'Extravagantly generous with her money, handing out cash and cheques to anyone who seemed in need of help ...'[64]

Forty years earlier, as Charles William Day wrote in his *Hints on Etiquette and the Usages of Society*, 'It is generally the misfortune of musical people to be such enthusiasts that they seldom know when to leave off. The listeners get fidgety and tired, although they are usually too polite to say so. A song now and then is very desirable, as it is a relief to conversation, but half a dozen consecutively would become a bore.'[65] Perhaps that attitude was still there in George's time, and only a Royal presence would change the behaviour.

Over the course of the 1850s to the 1870s the professionalisation of musicians had led to the appearance of pianists at all kinds of venues. Adaptability was the key to success, and George proved himself in that. It must be observed that George's habit with regard to his creativity was one of inviting the Muse in, rather that waiting for her to call. One of the most important collaborations in his career was to happen just at this time when he was branching out, with his confidence ascendant. This happened in 1876 when he met Florence Marryat. In his memoir, he glosses over how and when they met and simply writes: 'In 1876 Miss Florence Marryat, the novelist and daughter of the celebrated Capt. Marryat and I talked over a joint entertainment. It was quite apparent that the literary institutions were not what they were. Their fees, like their engagements, were rapidly decreasing.'[66]

The meeting happened not by chance, but after introductions by George Dolby, who was again making things happen. He was very good at doing that. The result of his work in this instance was a very exciting and original pairing of talents. As Beth Palmer wrote of Florence Marryat, 'Marryat's life did not fit any pre-conceived pattern for respectable feminine behaviour' – and that is a considerable understatement.[67] When she met and began her work with George, she was 43 but had packed so much into her life that her learning curve must have already peaked: she had attempted almost everything in the literary world, including editing, writing fiction and biography. She was born in 1833, one of eleven children of Captain Marryat, the famous novelist; by 1854 she was married to Thomas Ross Church, living with him in Malaya and later returning to England where she wrote to feed the family (as her husband was on half pay then), at first writing fiction stemming from the 'sensation novels' of the 1860s, and then editing the journal, *London Society.*

By the time she started her acting career in the mid-1870s, she had established herself as the leader of a circle of writers and illustrators around *London Society* and had also written *The Life and Letters of Captain Marryat* in 1872. She had acquired that toughness and resolution that comes of hardship; writing while nursing and bringing up her large family, and turning her hand to a number of markets and genres, demonstrating the multi-tasking essential to a literary professional at the time. If we add to this the fact that she was a woman in male-dominated literary and publishing world, then admiration grows still further.

In one of those intriguing ironies in the footnotes of literary history, it is worth noting that Florence was one the first editors to publish the young Bram Stoker: his story 'The Crystal Cup' appeared in an 1872 issue. Four years later, when Henry Irving was in Dublin with Bateman's company, Florence and George were also touring, and they went to one of Irving grand parties – at which Bram Stoker was present. As Tony Joseph has pointed out, George had a very enjoyable time in Dublin, although he did have an accident in the street when he fell off a vehicle and landed in mud. [68]

Someone of Florence's nature would have relished collaborating with George, who was sparkling, entertaining company, with the repartee and wit he had inherited from his father. Florence had also had the help of Dolby, who quite obviously knew 'horses for courses' where bookings, management and audiences were concerned. He must have sensed that these two would perform well together.

George wrote a sketch called *Cups and Saucers*, and this became the main element in an entertainment they called *Entre Nous,* in which songs, comedy in costume and impersonations formed something very close to a variety act with a dash of sophistication. But also, at the heart of this, there was the sheer inane fun that George relished, and *Cups and Saucers* was to become a curtain-raiser for the later work with D'Oyly Carte at the Opera Comique. The sketch is a perfect template to look at in order to grasp where the Grossmith humour lies.

The success of *Cups and Saucers* lay in the future, and its reception on stage was limited at first, but George thought a great deal of it in itself, as something he created as an expression of his own individual sense of gentle commentary on social types and fads.[69] We can see how and why it came into its own later as a curtain raiser, if we bear in mind the nature of those pieces, as described by W J MacQueen-Pope:

'This was a one-act play, seen only by the early-comers. It would play to empty boxes, half-empty upper circle, to a gradually filling stalls and dress circle, but to an attentive, grateful and appreciative pit and gallery. Often these plays were little gems. They deserved much better treatment than they got, but those who saw them delighted in them … They served to give young actors and actresses a chance to win their spurs …'[70]

But assuredly, it was 'a little gem.' One section of dialogue, which clearly foreshadows the Noel Coward treatment of deliberate absurd flatness, shows the tone of the piece. This is in which General Deelah and Emily Worcester, china maniacs, discuss the weather:

General: How fine it was today.
Mrs W: It was.
General: It was.
Mrs W: Yes, it was. (Pause)
General: And yet yesterday was wet.
Mrs W: (quickly) Yes it was. (Another pause)
General: Have you ever noticed –
Mrs W: Oh, I have!
General: So have I, frequently! How much we are alike.
But although the rain is disagreeable, yet I always think it

makes the grass and the fields and the flowers look – look wet.[71]

Florence and George went 'on the road' with their show, and in her book, *Tiddler's Ground*, Florence had stories of George and his antics during their travels, so he took the opportunity to recall some adventures on the tour. In Cardiff, she was taken ill and once again, George's network of friends and contacts saved the day. A local character called Courtenay Clarke stepped in and he assumed the role of comedian and master of ceremonies.. Clarke was well-known around Cardiff. Just a month earlier he had been part of the performance given by Signor Boz at a 'dark séance' given by this character at the Royal Hotel. This Boz had nothing to do with Dickens: he was a man strapped to a chair, in a dark atmosphere, with instruments and other objects placed nearby on a table, and then supposedly, he played the instruments and did tricks with the objects from his chair. Clarke was there as one of the witnesses, the audience seeing a woman's glove mysteriously go across the room to stop on Clarke's chest. Clarke was a literary man, and he had known George the First. He was reported as taking part, as president of the Cardiff Literary Club, in a meeting later that year when the topic was 'The Comparative Merits of Thackeray and Dickens.'

In *Tiddler's Ground* we have an anecdote which shows the sheer fun and high jinks around the pair on the road; Florence recalls staying at a hotel where the two went to their separate rooms. In Florence's room all was well until someone in the next room began to sing. She complained to the management and a formidable lady went to remonstrate with the noisy offender. This was the result next morning:

'The next morning when I met George Grossmith at the breakfast table, I perceived that he looked uneasy, as if he had something to communicate. As soon as he could speak without being overheard by the waiter, he said, "I got into such a scrape last night. I was preparing to go to bed and singing My Little Saucer to myself, when suddenly a door into my room opened and I saw a vision of some gaunt female, who slammed it again in my face. Presently in came the landlord who demanded what had I done to insult the lady in the next room ...'[72]

One of the best insights into the friendship of George and Florence on the road is the account of George at a paranormal table-tipping with Florence; he did not take the situation seriously, but Florence had a genuine interest in such studies. His banter and humour were annoying to her. A personage named 'Sticks' came through and communicated with knocks, but George's response was far from fair:

> 'The table was seized with convulsions and wriggled and oscillated to a corner of the room. When it was quiet I said, "Mr Sticks, I do not wish to be disrespectful, but are you drunk now?" Then came three solemn but distinct tilts. Miss Marryat considered I was most discourteous to poor Sticks and has never since sat with me at a table, except for lunch or dinner.'[73]

Florence and George were clearly kindred spirits. Both were – though this expressed itself very differently in them – artists with boundless energy and tremendous *joie de vivre*.

In George's case, the always essential factor of adapting to survive in the precarious business of performance and the theatrical life was something he could handle, being multi-talented, but even his versatility drops into second place by the side of Florence, whose energy, if captured and generated, could have provided power for a large city; when she wasn't writing fiction she was editing or child-rearing, and somehow in between this, she became a personality in the theatrical world as well.

Florence Marryat's work at the *London Society* magazine includes ample evidence of her deep interest in the theatrical society of the time: the features in that journal reflect the extent to which the fascination with stage celebrities was prominent in culture. Her features includes such topics as 'Notes on Popular Actresses' and 'Before the Footlights or Sketches of Playhouse Society.' There was also a series on fêtes – charity events involving the theatre personalities in vogue – and in one of these reports, we have a glimpse of the popularity (and indeed celebrity status) of someone who was to give George a great deal of help and advice in his coming change of career as he stepped from the world of penny readings and polytechnic entertaining onto the stage proper: Mrs Howard Paul. Florence's piece in the magazine includes this:

'Here we are then, once more in the great transept of the Crystal Palace, purchasing pin-cushions from pretty actresses in the cause of charity ... It was most gratifying to observe that the old favourites obtained the largest share of patronage ... There was no getting a glimpse of Mrs Mellen, Mrs Paul or Mrs Rowe for the eager crowds which thronged around them all day long to pay homage to their worth no less than to their talents.'[74]

This is a genuine insight into the cultural interest in the social world of actors and acting: a sidelight on the clamour for meeting and knowing the stars of the stage at a time when audiences were massive, not only at the music halls but at the fringe performances, the theatres and halls in which smaller-scale productions were on offer. It was an age in which pictures and cards of the stars were beginning to be on sale, and the cult of celebrity was soon to be escalated by the arrival of photography as a part of the publicity machine.

Mrs Paul was destined to step in when George most needed help to move from fringe entertainer and jack-of-all-trades to comic opera lead role.

But just before that revolution in the Grossmith family fortunes, the young married man could see that his financial security was far from assured. In fact, he was worried. He wrote in his memoir, 'After entertaining all over the country for seven years, I made a rather important discovery: viz., that my income was as rapidly decreasing each year as my house and family expenses were increasing.' [75]

This can easily be understood when a summary of his situation is noted: when he sat back and reflected on the precarious nature of his life as a strolling player, he already had one son, GG, who had been born in 1874, and Rosa was pregnant with Lawrence (they would later also have two daughters, Cordelia and Sylvia). His income was not only moderate but unpredictable, and what was looming was the prospect of the life of the touring player – seasonal and gruelling. But there was a more threatening aspect too: the thought of his particular act being finite in its span of interest. In other words, he could never be sure that Scarborough or Leamington would want him back a second or a third time. Variety was the essence of the profession, unless you were a special, major star.

On a more personal and emotional level, touring meant being estranged from the family. Too many actors on the road saw much too little of their loved ones. It was a life for a single person. There is no doubt that George had been reared in the bosom of a loving family, one with all the small-scale chaos and mess of a full, vivacious lifestyle, with George the First as a paterfamilias who pretended to be stern but really lavished affection on his children, relishing their success in the arts when it happened, but backing them in whatever they did. Then, at this crossroads in George's life, came the letter which was to change his life forever. It arrived in November 1877:

'Beefsteak Club King William Street Tuesday night
Dear Mr Grossmith – are you inclined to go on the stage for a time? There is a part in the new piece I am doing with Gilbert which I think you would play admirably. I can't find a good man for it. Let me have a line, or come to 9, Albert mansions tomorrow after 4 or Thursday before 2.30
Yours sincerely,
Arthur Sullivan'[76]

3

WORKING FOR GILBERT AND
SULLIVAN

'A wandering minstrel I, a thing of shreds and patches.'
W S Gilbert: *The Mikado*

In the late 1860s the great composer of operettas, Jacques Offenbach, became hugely successful in London. It had not been a rapid process. As Peter Gammond has written, '... the English-speaking world's Offenbach craze was a delayed action affair ... mainly as a result of the dilettante attitude of British producers, directors and writers.' [77]

But the éclat was great indeed. The influence of French musical theatre was to bring about one of the main impulses behind the attitudes and aspirations of Arthur Sullivan. He was recorded as saying, in a later interview, that he never wanted his stage music to be like the 'French school' with its 'gaudy and tinsel tunes.'[78]

Gilbert and Sullivan, coming together to produce *Trial by Jury* at the Royalty Theatre in 1875, had teamed up with the impresario Richard D'Oyly Carte, and at the time Sullivan wrote his momentous letter quoted at the end of the previous chapter, to George, inviting him to come to an audition, they were planning a very English full-length work. *Trial by Jury* had been in some ways a taster and a tester for them, and it had proved a success. In the face of European influence, they wanted to use specifically English characters, settings and themes; they seem to have been slightly in line with the kind of thought later adopted by Percy Grainger, with his notions of 'blue-eyed English.' In early 1876, the duo received a generous advance of 200 guineas from D'Oyly Carte, given with Gilbert's next project in mind. That was to be *The Sorcerer*, and hence the search for the light baritone, and the letter to George, after he had been 'scouted' for the role. George's first major role was to be that of John Wellington Wells, of the family firm of sorcerers at the centre of the tale.

Gilbert always had his finger on the pulse. In 1877, when he developed *The Sorcerer* from one of his published stories, 'An Elixir of Love' which had appeared in *The Graphic* in 1876, the clash of scientific rationalism and spiritual beliefs was very much in the intellectual sphere as a subject of debate. Within the previous ten years there had been high-profile cases in which this conflict of opinions came out for full combat in the press and in learned talks and meetings. The 'cunning folk,' who were often quack doctors, in working-class cultures still persisted and a belief in folklore and the paranormal was always there, in popular cultural narratives.[79]

In spite of Gilbert's longing to create topsy-turvydom settings and storylines of the simplicity of pantomime and burlesque, the appeal of the new Gilbert and Sullivan form of theatre was one of mild satire, impersonations and parodies of fads and vogues.

In this context, George arrived at his new destination: stage star. It had been engineered by Sullivan, who had seen George at work, but was also very much due to Mrs Howard Paul, who advised him to take the opportunity, unlike his father who did not recommend the new career. George explains this in his memoir, quoting the letter from Mrs Paul in which she wrote to him: ' It is a splendid part – better than you think I fancy – and the patter song is great in its way. Make your time suit them or theirs suit you … Don't think me impertinent in writing this, but I want to see your name in the cast …'[80]

She had been cast as Lady Sangazure, and of course she knew George's abilities very well. Her experience had taught her to understand the workings of the profession, and she realised that George was only on the margins, not actually part of the great family of stage performers. But he was waiting in the wings, and he took her advice. Being George, he was adept at having fun at his own expense, writing that one of the directors of the Comedy Opera Company (D'Oyly Carte's financial backers) had written to Carte, 'Whatever you do, don't engage Grossmith.'[81]

When George had a meeting with Sullivan, before matters were finalised, he went with doubts about his ability to sing to the standard required. He recalled that, as he sat with Sullivan, the composer 'struck the D … and said, "sing it out; as loud as you can." I did. Sullivan looked, with a most humorous expression on his face – even his eye-glass seemed to smile.'[82] George then sang the line from his part as Wells, 'My name is John Wellington Wells' and the rest is history. He was the man they wanted.

The Sorcerer, and the short story on which it was based, is about the effects of a love philtre on the residents of the little village of

Ploverleigh. The Gilbert method is to take one plain storyline and embellish in a variety of ways, at different levels, so that once the audience have entered the theatre and given in to that 'willing suspension of disbelief' that theatre requires, their responses are to be worked and mined so that play and high-jinks may follow. It was produced at the Opera Comique, which was by the Strand, and was to last until 1904. Everything depended on the casting, and along with George came other notable acquisitions to the great Gilbert and Sullivan enterprise, including Rutland Barrington as Dr Daly. Barrington, like George, was to become a real Savoyard celebrity, and in his memoirs he explained the importance of the experience: 'What halcyon days for managements! And who can wonder at the fortunes amassed, and justly, by the great triumvirate? For after all they took a certain risk in letting loose on London a band of artists some of whom had never before been heard of.'[83]

Barrington also adds that everyone connected with the show was proud to feel English, and that some people with Italian names adapted accordingly; he was being amusing and going for a cheap laugh, one feels, but there is an element in *The Sorcerer* in which Gilbert's skill with throwaway lines and slick jokes reach out for a very English self-directed humour, as here, when Mr Wells (George) says of his firm's sale of 'Superior Blessings': 'We've only sold one since Christmas – to a gentleman who bought it to send to his mother-in-law – but it turned out that he was afflicted in the head, and it's been returned on our hands.'[84]

In the opera, Wells appears well into the action of the first act, after plenty of singing and reflection about the worth of true love and constancy: a scene illustrated in *The Illustrated London News* for 23 February 1878 shows something of the nature of how Wells has to move, along with the stage effect of burning coals. The part was absolutely ideal for George. After all, he was a master of the narrative song which incorporated shifts in intonation; physical as well as verbal humour; and most of all, the range of skills involved in what we know as 'patter.' The entrance of Wells in *The Sorcerer* entails a lengthy patter song with changes in its metrical basis, so that Wells' account of his profession of sorcerer structures the changes of movement and mood that Grossmith had to put into the piece. Gilbert's favourite measures are there – from the AABBA stanza (of the limerick) to his beloved trimester stanzas with rapidly delivered syllables and Latinate vocabulary in the end-rhymes.

The patter song is a mix of audience rapport and musical movement: the metrical forms Gilbert liked for this open up all kinds of potential for the player's delivery, and Gilbert was meticulous in orchestrating the sequence of words and actions. The constant problem for the artists working with him was the issue of the 'ad lib.' George explains this:

'The musical rehearsals are child's play in comparison with the stage rehearsals.Mr Gilbert is a perfect autocrat, insisting that his words should be delivered, even to an inflection of the voice, as he dictates. He will stand on the stage beside the actor or actress, and repeat the words with appropriate action over and over again, until they are delivered as he desires them to be. In some instances of course, he allows a little licence, but very little.'[85]

The fact is that such direction would not be too much of a challenge for George. A reflection on his established artistic habits should note that an act relying on mimicry and impersonation, or at least the adoption of a certain class-defined voice, relies on a somewhat mechanical method, one lending itself to the tight control attained in practice and repetition. The rehearsals for the Opera Comique must have been close to the kinds of professional habits George had already cultivated. The main difference, however, was that he was now rather a mannequin in other hands, losing autonomy. But in the opening patter song of *The Sorcerer* it is clear that there was ample room for his personality, in spite of the close direction behind the delivery of the lines. Within the metrically formed lines, he could still shift intonation to match any meaningful glances or movements, as in 'There's no cheaper house in the trade/ love philtre – we've quantities of it;' where any monotone expression simply to use a rhyme would miss the chance of a parody of advertising phrases.

What all this means is that, in short, George Grossmith, society entertainer and itinerant performer, had found his metier. In his first role of Wells, there is no doubt that he was the main attraction: there is plenty of fun in the brief encounters of those in love with what they see when they open their eyes after taking the philtre, but in the conglomeration of arias and duets the character of Wells invariably stays in the limelight, notably when Lady Sangazure (Mrs Paul) sees Wells 'and becomes fascinated with him' as the direction has it. Their duet is gloriously charming, with the woman repeating 'Love me' and Wells replying with 'hate me' so that Gilbert's wit is allowed to spin from the mundane to the sheer surreal of lines such as: 'Hate me! I often roll down One Tree Hill!'(referring to Honor Oak in Lewisham), and also he adds a line which is part of the overall content and topical bite of the Savoy operas – 'Hate me! I sometimes go to Rosherville!' with the response, 'Love me! That joy I'll share.' The reference had been used before in the 1866 comic piece by Sullivan and Burnand, *Cox and Box*. The reference was to an immensely popular pleasure-trip down the Thames to the Rosherville gardens in Gravesend, Kent, and clearly Gilbert was pointedly alluding to the popular culture of what his audience would think of as 'the masses'. There was a terrible irony, too, as less than a year after the last performance of *The Sorcerer*, there was one of the worst disasters of Victorian England as the *Princess Alice* paddle-steamer capsized after leaving the pier for Rosherville.

The production lasted for 175 performances, and as Leslie Baily has written, its success was a template for things to come: 'It was the solid base on which Gilbert and Sullivan were to build their absurd castles of fantasy for the next twenty years.'[86] Its reception was enthusiastic and generally responsive to the fruits of a collaboration which was patently one with a bright future. *The Times* wrote that Sullivan's orchestration was outstanding: '... he is thoroughly acquainted with every resource of that important element in dramatic music, it need scarcely be added that it is invariably used with pointed and well-considered effect ...'[87]

In a lengthy section of his memoirs, Grossmith is more concerned to tell anecdotes of other actors and to extract the comic value of his own learning-curve as the star of the succession of shows that were to follow *The Sorcerer*. But he does tell us a great deal about the material, everyday professional business of the actor/singer as he understood it, and these insights illuminate his methods and his thinking behind the kind of performance values he developed. For instance, there is the matter of make-up, which he explains with reference to a question he was often asked about whether or not he did his own:

'No-one has ever touched my face but myself. I select
my own colours, powders, rouges, and try several effects
of complexions before finally deciding on one. I have a
little dressing-room to myself – the only one who has at

the Savoy ... I do not think the painted lines on the face should ever be seen, even from the stalls.'[88]

Horace Hutchinson, writer and golfer (known as 'the father of golf instruction') wrote in his book on cultural figures of the 1880s, an impression of Grossmith and Rutland Barrington, and his account vividly explains how well they worked together, as is perhaps typified in their playing of the Captain and Sir Joseph Porter in *HMS Pinafore*:

'Each was just made to be the other's fool ... Anything more waspish than the thinness and fragility of Grossmith it is impossible to conceive. Perhaps it should be gnat-ish rather than waspish. He did not suggest a creature with any envenomed sting, but rather a restless, buzzing thing, ever about your head, ever ready to give you pin-pricks. He would dart and dance over the solid bulk of Barrington in all directions, bewilderingly agile; Barrington standing unmoved and unruffled the while. It was like the encounter of Dignity and Impudence. I think in The Mikado he had developed the faculty of sitting down into the cross-legged tailor's attitude with a suddenness that was scarcely human and scarcely like a living thing at all: more like the action reversed of a jack-in-the-box.'[89]

This conveys very well the images we have of George from the various drawings in the illustrated periodicals when they reviewed the productions: he looks very wiry and thin. Everything in the figures depicted suggests energy and athleticism. Hutchinson's description also suggests to us today a pairing very much like Abbott and Costello or Laurel and Hardy. Barrington had that Falstaffian quality of stolidity, contrasted with George's constant movement.

George in this time of great success was experiencing a revolution in his life: the family were now living in Blandford Square, Marylebone, where they had settled in 1874, and on 11 May that year, GG was born. When the flush of success led Gilbert and Sullivan to produce *HMS Pinafore* in 1878, George was beginning to create that full and vivacious home life for his family, just as his father had done before. As GG grew up in the 1880s, he was to experience not only to experience a paterfamilias who led an exciting celebrity lifestyle; he also felt the sheer wonderment of the expanding social circle around George. GG wrote later, when he himself was a stage star, 'And yet what a wonderful home and what wonderful people passed through its doors! Great singers, artists, musicians, writers, judges, princes and poets ...' GG also makes a point that invites us to reflect on George and Rosa from another perspective, perhaps something which happened as a result of Freemasonry connections: 'Occasionally my parents would specialize ... It would be my mother's evening – scientists, theologists and her special pets, theosophists, as well as many charming people not in the public eye.'[90]

There was not much from the whole, fascinating spectrum of Victorian life in the last decades of the century that did not have a place in the conversations in Blandford Square. Rosa was obviously, as so many were at the time, intrigued by Theosophy. Helena Blavatsky and H S Olcott has formed the Theosophy Society in 1875 and Blavatsky came to live in London in 1887. Her book, *The Secret Doctrine*, was published in 1888, and her talk of her beliefs – defined as 'the archaic wisdom-religion' with an aspiration towards a brotherhood and sisterhood of humanity – would have appealed to the Grossmiths, who were so communal-minded that the twentieth-century word 'socialite' applies very well to them.

In the late 1870s, George had 'arrived' – largely due to the phenomenal success of *HMS Pinafore*, the follow-up to *The Sorcerer*. This celebrity status may be gleaned, for example, from his place in a compendium written by Charles Eyre Pascoe, *The Dramatic List* of 1879. Here his biographical entry includes an account of his earlier performances and then adds: 'In May 1878 he became connected with H M S Pinafore as Sir Joseph Porter K C B., a character sustained by him in a spirit of the most refined and amusing burlesque. During the 'run' of that piece Mr Grossmith has composed several drawing room comic songs of a popular character ...'[91]

This is clear evidence that George was still working as hard as ever to do his own thing, as well as being Gilbert's star turn. One trait we find recurring throughout George's autobiographical writings is his concern for money – for financial security. His worry about losing a steady income has already been noted, as he accepted the offer to appear on the stage at the Opera Comique; the inference has to be made that he was sustaining his private work and his hallmark piano entertainment not only for pleasure but for a secondary income. This was definitely to pay dividends. He kept this up through the next twenty years, and after one of his last tours, in 1900, he made

£20,000 from a two-year run, all based on his 'Piano and I' routines. In today's values (2013) that would be over £1,200,000.

Early in his Gilbert and Sullivan career he was still, naturally, maintaining his club life; in 1881 the Savage Club moved from Covent Garden to the Savoy Hotel. Albert Edward, Prince of Wales, was a member, and in 1882 he was there when a dinner was held at the club's 25th anniversary at Willis' rooms in Covent Garden, at which George was present along with Arthur Sullivan and the painter, Frederick Leighton.

There is here, as with so much in the lives of actors and singers, the familiar situation of the lacunae, the gaps, of knowledge in the records. The facts – events and appearances – are plentiful, but to move closer to seeing George's more personalised reactions to this dizzying new life, we have to use surmise and a rather empathic angle on matters. There is no doubt that he had learned all the social skills from his parents, and he had acquired great charm. In the portraits and sketches, there is an openness in his face, a profound intelligence; we have the feeling that here was a man who delighted in conviviality, but equally, his habit of always looking on the bright side had gone deeper: he was always likely to 'send up' a situation, and it would be fair to say that, in most things, there was not a serious bone in his body. Yet that would be a lop-sided view of course; the implication of such comment would be that he may have been one-sided and predictable, perhaps cultivating that attitude to fend off stress and anxiety. There is some truth in that. But still the question remains: was his constant identity as a 'personality' in total contrast to the role he played at home, as a father? From GG's memories it would seem wise to say no to that. He is everywhere recorded as being approachable, charming and easy-going. When GG recalls that George was apparently strict, one feels that it was always in a spirit of play, or at least of purposeful drama to amuse as well as to direct. This may be seen in GG's story of his father's reaction to Gilbert wanting GG to make his debut: 'My father had always been the most generous of parents, never denying me anything within reason, but on this occasion he pointed a stern finger at me and said, Now you can earn your own living. Don't ever again ask me for a penny.'

The impact of *HMS Pinafore* in 1878 was phenomenal: everyone concerned in the Gilbert and Sullivan enterprise found themselves part of a huge success; Gilbert had prepared the piece methodically, going to Portsmouth and spending time on board *Victory*, sketching and making notes, and of course, talking to sailors, to absorb the authentic sense of language he needed. He even had the costumes for the production made by a tailor to the fleet. The work had a truly British appeal, as the salts on board her Majesty's ships were crucial to the preservation of the Empire across the seas. In fact, as the production was in process, they were preparing for a vital part in the African campaigns that would soon lead to the momentous battles with the Zulu, as gunboats from the British navy played a part in that war. But there was much more in terms of the context, particularly in the usual topicality.

Sir Joseph Porter, commander of the Queen's navy, was George's role, and his famous song recounting his rise to that office was a clear reference to the fact that the entrepreneur W H Smith was First Lord – an appointment made by Benjamin Disraeli. The lines,

> 'Stick close to your desk and never go to sea,
> And you all may be rulers of the Queen's navy'

were of course a powerful satire.

Both Gilbert and Sullivan were ill during the writing of the piece; Sullivan had a liver complaint, and Gilbert was suffering the onset of gout, and he also had backache. Yet nothing was to stop the work going ahead, and the opening night was on 25 May 1878 at the Opera Comique, with all the right ingredients for a massive triumph. After all, it was all about love between the classes, in a society of rigid social hierarchy. If we combine that with some of the brightest and most memorable one-liners, jokes and songs, then no more explanation is needed. After this interchange between the Captain and chorus, all of London was saying the lines, with a smile:

> Capt: I am never known to quail
> At the fury of a gale
> And I'm never, never sick at sea!
> All: What never?
> Capt: No, never.
> All: What, *never*?
> Capt: Hardly ever.

George's light baritone was fine for the patter and the interplay as well; his Sir Joseph Porter was ideal for the humour arising from the contrast with the large Rutland Barrington, and in addition, there was the appearance of Jessie Bond as Hebe, Sir Joseph's cousin. This led to wonderful duets and trios, and in the 'Never mind the why and wherefore' song it is not difficult to imagine the stage business of George and Rutland, with contrasting movements as they worked the piece for every laugh, orchestrated, of course, by Gilbert's precise direction.

The whole business was very demanding work. George described the rehearsals, and to add to that we have the testimony of others present that working with the great team and their directors was tough in the extreme. George Power, who was the tenor singing the part of Ralph Rackstraw, described some of the stress when he was interviewed for *The Era*:

'It was a wonder some of us appeared "on the night" at all. On the very day before the production, I remember, we rehearsed hard from 11 to 4. Then we had some down, we had a bite of supper, and began the full dress rehearsal of H M S Pinafore. This was over at about four o'clock in the morning. All the time, the old directors were stamping up and down, utterly dissatisfied. "Call this wit?" they exclaimed. "Call this comic opera?"'[92]

Jessie Bond had very little to do as Hebe, and Harriet Everard stole the female limelight as Little Buttercup. Yet Jessie was later to become a celebrity, and her memoirs provide a very good source for George's life on stage; she had experienced most of the torments and challenges that life could throw at you, recovering from smallpox (which few did); being forced into a marriage, and perhaps the worst suffering of all, an abscess on her leg which never really healed throughout her acting career with Gilbert and Sullivan.

She was only twenty-five when Gilbert recruited her, and had been prominent in several contexts, including singing at the benefit concert for the Pauls at the Queen's Hall in Liverpool. When Cellier's short piece, *After All*, was later added to *Pinafore*, she sang in that. Later in her career, she teamed up to do a duo act with Rutland Barrington. Looking at the many pictures of her in studio photos and in promotional illustrations, it is easy to see why she was a natural for the soubrette mezzo-soprano roles.

The production was destined to be the focus of one of George's most dramatic experiences – but not in a theatrical sense: in fact, there was an unseemly brawl in the midst of the action. Jessie Bond wrote an account of what happened:

'On the last night of the old regime the angry directors – who by the way had only put down five hundred pounds to start with – came to the stage door with vans and furniture removers who rushed in and tried to carry away the scenery, which the directors claimed as their own property. The performance was nearly over; Miss Everard was singing at the time, and she pluckily tried to continue her part, in spite of the noise going on behind the scenes, and heard all over the house. There was no panic, though the startled audience suspected fire, and a few people left the theatre. Alfred Cellier had to stop the orchestra, Frank Thornton ran around the box and spoke to the people …'[93]

George then came forward and did the most sensible thing: he explained what was happening. Fear of fire was the main worry, as fires in theatres were common, mainly because of the gas heating and lighting, and of course, risks from smokers' habits. George's long experience of dealing with every kind of audience came through to help matters. Yet there was still a brawl.

The cause of all this was that during the long summer heat-wave of 1879, when the audiences had dropped markedly and the whole enterprise was under threat of closure, the directors of the Comedy Opera Company invested £500 each. Amazingly, when receipts dipped further, they decided to pull out completely and start another company. Consequently, they wanted all their property and decided to grab it. On 31 July, as Jessie and the rest were in mid-performance, there was a fight on stage behind them. Sir George Power has described it: 'There was a free fight of considerable fierceness. The intruders rushed down the narrow staircase leading to the stage, and as quick as lightning our stage hands were summoned to keep them back. The two parties met on the stairs. The struggle lasted more than an hour …'[94]

The directors appeared in the dock at Bow Street, so either George himself or his father would have been writing up the report for *The Times*. Whoever wrote the piece, the result was a masterpiece of precision, as it was noted that the directors were prosecuted for causing a riot and for assault on a certain Mr Barker. Prosecuting was the colourful and charismatic lawyer, Montagu Williams, who requested that the summons be withdrawn because the gentlemen had met in a friendly manner since the first hearing. However, two of the directors wanted to make sure that the court heard their grievance, as the report closed with, 'Mr Bailey and Mr Chappell did all they could to avert a disturbance, which was the last thing dreamt of by them when they went down, under legal advice, to claim what they believed they were entitled to.'[95] In other words, they were saying that entering the theatre during the performance and carrying off property by force was not provocative. Amazingly, Mr Flowers, the Bow Street magistrate, well known to George in his law-reporting work, had to concede that the accused had satisfied the court that no breach of peace was intended. One has to wonder whether or not there were Masonic brothers involved here. But whatever the nature of the compromise, George was involved, and as Tony Joseph has pointed out, in a bizarre way. He was called as a witness to give an account of the neglect of the drains at the theatre during the long hot summer. He was sure that 'the moment the receipts went down the drains got into a bad condition … He had special reasons for being positive.' One imagines his father sitting and watching George comment on matters which really required the testimony of a plumber.[96]

The result of all this was that a new company was formed, with Gilbert, Sullivan and Carte working together, and each one gave £1,000 as trading capital. This was done in the midst of what has been called 'Pinafore mania.' The show was such a success that other companies wanted a share of the profits, and in America, rival productions were staged. The natural manoeuvre for the new partners was to take a company across and do their own show, making it clear that all rivals were poor shadows of the real thing. The experience taught them to take care when planning the next opera, and Gilbert was fully aware of the copyright issues. It was an easy matter at the time to take the formula for success of any show and do another version. Gilbert's next piece, *The Pirates of Penzance*, was going to be produced in such a way that there would be a degree of protection and a thoughtful progression in controlling the shows as much as possible. Where this led was to a distinctive feature of the whole Gilbert and Sullivan enterprise: to have a company in London and a company on the move. It was an idea that reflected the military system of having regiments at home and abroad, with the exception that the star line-up would be in London – or in other capitals later, of course.

The sheer chaos and panic caused by the pirated productions of *Pinafore* highlights the parlous situation that writers and playwrights were in at this time with regard to their intellectual property. In fact, just a few years after the debacle over *Pinafore*, the second version of the Society of Authors was formed (the first having been created in 1843), and Gilbert was a member, but the situation before that was simply disastrous for anyone trying to protect artistic rights. There had been a Royal Commission on Copyright, chaired by Lord Manners, in 1875, and in its report there was an explanation of the ineffective state of the law in these matters:

> 'The first observation which a study of the existing
> law suggests is that its form, as distinguished from its
> substance, seems to us bad. The law is wholly destitute of
> any sort of arrangement, incomplete, often obscure, and
> even when it is intelligible on long study, it is in many
> parts so ill-expressed that no-one who does not give such
> study to it can expect to understand it.' [97]

The main recommendation regarding the protection of dramatists' work was that when a work was published, that fact should create copyright protection for its performance. But what exactly constituted a 'dramatic entertainment' was vague; there was also exploitation of writers in all contexts and in all the sites of mediation and promotion of artistic work. But things were changing, and in 1884 at the momentous meeting at which Tennyson was made President of the new Society of Authors, Gilbert spoke with the hard lessons of experience behind him when he contributed to the debate: 'Responding for drama, Gilbert said that critics, managers and the public were indisposed or unable to distinguish adequately between original works which cost the author seven or eight months' careful intellectual preparation and French three-act indecencies which did not cost a week's mental labour.'[98]

While the world was in the throes of '*Pinafore* mania', Gilbert was at work on his *Pirates* script. George was firmly established as the lead male 'character' as opposed to the romantic lead, and the method Gilbert had created – what Leslie Baily describes as 'to treat a thoroughly farcical subject in a thoroughly serious manner'[99] – was ideal for George's ability to immerse himself into the roles, thoroughly understanding the need to make the most of each set-piece patter. As *HMS Pinafore* illustrates very well, the key to Gilbert and Sullivan's art in their new operas was in the absolute appeal to fundamental British popular culture at a time of great social flux. One of George's anecdotes shows Gilbert's attitude here. He writes of one actress, who played Josephine, pointing out to Gilbert that in Italian opera she would always stand centre-stage. He goes on: 'Gilbert said, most persuasively, "Oh but this is not Italian opera; this is only a low burlesque of the worst possible kind." Gilbert says this sort of thing in such a serious way that one scarcely knows whether he is joking or not.'[100]

George could not resist concocting an absurd situation – in life, as in theatre. His own autobiography is a string of dramatic incidents, many of which he created in order to extract humour, and to have a laugh at others' expense. If we add to that one of the most distinctive aspects of the Gilbert characters he played – the contemporary pastiche – then it can be seen just how at home he felt in the great roles he played. He was to find that in his next character – the Major General in *The Pirates of Penzance*. In George's piano acts, he had revelled in presenting 'types' and he based these on what he saw or read about. In this new role, the clear reference was to General Wolseley. In 1875 the Hartington Commission recommended a War Office department with a Chief of Staff whose business would be largely that of collecting information. In fact, in the person of Wolseley this kind of function had begun, as he set about creating a fresh breed of officer and placed military intelligence within a generally more forward-looking and educated elite of senior staff. However, although the new Branch was initially under Sir John Ardagh's command, at the time of its formation Wolseley was in West Africa, leading the expeditionary force against the Ashanti, and this provides an enlightening case study in which we may see the new attitudes at work, particularly as Wolseley was destined to take over the Branch later. Wolseley, in the words of one of his biographers, saw that 'War was a serious business and soldiering a profession, not a pastime for dilettantes. The days of playing at soldiers were over. Education in the army, still at a dangerously low ebb, should permeate through all ranks.'[101]

Wolseley put the emphasis on gathering the right team of officers around him and then planned to use native fighters, with a request to the high command that regular troops would be ready to arrive if needed. He even gave his superiors a quote for the job, of £150,000. Wolseley also involved the navy, for diplomatic reasons, and so the force that eventually arrived and set about marching on Kumasi, the Ashanti main settlement, was a mixed one in which some of the fiercest African warriors were travelling along with a naval detachment and Fanti people. But Wolseley realised, at a later stage of planning, that he would need some professionals from Britain and he had no less a force than the Black Watch with him.

Wolseley had officers whose task it was to survey local conditions and also to collect a viable force of local fighters. Indicative of the new thinking was the nature of the key men in the Wolseley team. There was Lieutenant Maurice, an instructor from Sandhurst; Captain Buller; Major Colley; and the future principal of the Intelligence Branch, the colourful Captain Brackenbury. But perhaps the most significant feature of the early phase of the Ashanti campaign was Garnet Wolseley's own habits; he studied blue books and reports assiduously and he worked his way through all the information about the place and people that he could find. As Joseph Lehmann noted: 'For the first time in the history of the British Empire, a general appointed to command an expedition sat down to a table at the War Office with the Secretary for War, the Secretary for the Colonies, the First Lord of the Admiralty and the various heads of military departments to discuss the necessary arrangements.'[102]

There was a library of books on topography and history available for the staff to peruse. Not to put too fine a point on it, this was *intelligent* intelligence in war. This kind of professional, rather lampooned in the press at times as a general who was at a desk administrating, lies behind the character George played next. These lines from one of the most sung and quoted patter-songs in *Pirates* shows how Sir Garnet fits the bill:

> 'For my military knowledge, though I'm plucky and adventury,
> Has only been brought down to the beginning of the century;
> But still in matters vegetable, animal and mineral,
> I am the very model of a modern Major GINeral!'

Gilbert had seen, in the success of *HMS Pinafore*, just how enthusiastically his public responded to the kind of satire that took, as its subject, basic aspects of Englishness, elements of the social order, and the Establishment, and so in his new piece there were several apposite targets for fun: not only the army, but the police were in focus this time.

The three men in the new company had to plan the next first night carefully, and there were openings on both sides of the Atlantic: a production in New York, and then the first British appearance of the opera at the Royal Bijou Theatre at Paignton in Devon, by the touring company. This strategy was to make sure that they had copyright, and so it was presented there for one day only, just after Christmas in 1879.

George and the usual company presented the first London staging on 3 April 1880 at the Opera Comique. Within a month, George had the terrible news of his father's death, and then, following swiftly after this, a salutary reminder that the work done for *The Times* at the Bow Street police court was likely to be a burden. He had farmed out the work to a deputy, John Cleverly, and after a particular report written by Cleverly about a solicitor called Bathurst was said to be false and defamatory, George had to take some action. The report in question had been syndicated and the editor of *The Morning Advertiser* was very much perturbed that 'no stigma should rest on any person representing his journal.'[103]

The hearing took place at the Marlborough Street court, and *The Times* report explained: 'Mr Cleverly stated that he was present in court when a case involving the detention of a coat came before Mr Flowers. A person named Currans was the complainant and Osborne the defendant. He wrote a short report of the case in the ordinary performance of his duties. There was no truth in the statement (the alleged libel) that the report was inserted in consequence of a bribe.'[104] Even more interesting here is that fellow entertainer Corney Grain defended Cleverly. He was, naturally, referred to in the proper way as 'Mr J P Grain.' George may have laughed this off later, but it is sensible to suggest that cases such as that were hardly likely to help in his current situation of stage personality and celebrity.

George the First had been giving an address at the Savage Club on 24 April when he was taken ill. He collapsed and Weedon ran to the theatre to tell George that their father was very ill. Three hours after his collapse, he died at the Club, with his brother ('the Young Roscius') and his sons by his side.

The death brings up one of the strangest and most incredible events in George's life. A messenger apparently went from the Club to George's mother at home and spoke these unbelievably callous words: 'I've come to tell you your husband's dead, here's the sausages we found in his pocket, and would you mind paying sixpence for having the handkerchief laundered one of the members put over his face.' As Tony Joseph rightly notes, 'The whole business left Grossmith himself agonisingly distressed.'[105]

The funeral was at Kensal Green cemetery. Letters of condolence flowed in from all kinds of places; George the First had a very wide circle of friends, and being a Mason, he had a considerable network of professional 'brothers.' George makes a special point of mentioning his father's reputation and popularity and also makes a personal statement – rare in his memoir of the time: 'If his loss was felt so much by people who only knew him slightly, what must it have been to his two sons who idolised the very ground he walked on ... His last lecture was at Wrexham ... and the kind clergyman who entertained him wrote one of the first and sweetest letters of sympathy that I received.'[106]

One poignant piece of family theatrical history is that George's uncle, William Robert Grossmith, was at the funeral; he had been 'The Infant Roscius' the theatrical prodigy as a child, at a time when such figures were lionised and widely reviewed, and he would have been in the shadow of the great William Betty (1791-1874), similarly dubbed 'The Young Roscius', the term being a generic one for a young actor. Uncle Robert lived until 1899, when he had reached the exceptional age of eighty-one.

Arthur Sullivan wrote a letter to George, referring to the 'great loss' but adding the very Victorian argument: 'I do honestly believe that a speedy return to the daily routine of one's life is the best distraction one can have in great trouble – distasteful as it may be to make the effort.'[107]

George returned to law reporting, and kept on assistants, including Cleverly, but it was just a matter of time before it became too much. After five more years, he finally stopped working for *The Times*. If we look at his lifestyle during the first few years of his stage career, there is no surprise that he contracted out the law reporting. He wrote that he played 200 consecutive nights of *The Sorcerer* and then 700 as Sir Joseph Porter in *Pinafore*. He had also never given up his 'society clown ' appearances at the piano, and his stories about being recognised on train journeys make it clear that he was a celebrity – a 'face' that people knew.

His performance as the Major General in *The Pirates of Penzance* was a huge success, and one that he shared with others, as there are so many colourful characters in the tale. Rutland Barrington explained his own success as the policeman, as he spoke about the 'Enterprising Burglar' song: 'It appeared in the second act ... it was such an immense success that I always had to repeat the last verse at least twice and in a rash moment I one day presumed to ask Gilbert to give me one. He informed me that *encore* meant *sing again*'[108], presumably a rebuke to Barrington for pretending he didn't know what 'encore' meant.

The reviews were enthusiastic, but Sullivan always felt that he was capable of 'better' and in the case of Gilbert, the serious playwright in him was always going to create mixed opinions.[109] Nevertheless, as far as George was concerned, the Major General was a marvellous part, with some undeniable scene-stealing *tour de force* songs, surely tempting for lots of ad libs, banned by Gilbert and the source of continuing disagreement between all the comics and the director/writer. As for Sullivan, he had managed to create music that everyone around London was humming, from cab drivers to lords. George Grossmith, 'society clown' was actually now a society hit – and a popular hit too.

He has very little to say about his performance, and about the nature of the role, in his memoirs; still, there is no difficulty in envisaging the spectacle: *The Era* reported that 'Genuine, eager, hearty, harmless fun must always be welcome, and the fun of *The Pirates of Penzance* is absolutely free from reproach.' The reviewer adds that there are many old favourites in the cast and praises as first among these:

> 'Mr George Grossmith junior *(sic)*, who makes of Major General Stanley one of the most amusing figures in the gallery of eccentric portraits, for which we are indebted to his wonderful skill in music and mimicry. Mr Grossmith has worked up the General's song, in which he has to stop at the end of a line to get a correct rhyme, until it is one of the very drollest items in the opera, and it has to be repeated every night; so comic and unexpected is this effect of the quaint lines Mr Gilbert has written for this part, rendered all the more ludicrous by the whimsically absent manner in which the performer tries to recall the lost or unknown rhyme and the ecstatic air with which he delivers it at last. This one song and the manner of its delivery would alone stamp Mr Grossmith as one of the very first of humorists in an original and eccentric school.'[110]

That has to be the best review George ever had. Not all critics grasped the nature of this new opera genre, somewhere between burlesque and satire, with a 'topsy-turvydom' so prominent in Gilbert's view of the world. *The Examiner*, for instance, had a columnist who wrote a series called 'The Theatre of Examiner' and he took a very po-faced and solemn angle on what was supposed to be light entertainment, making a strange and contradictory statement on George: 'Mr G. Grossmith plays the ridiculous major-General Stanley with the blandness and quietude that made the part tell so strongly on the opening night.' The same writer was a master of the back-handed compliment, asking whether the public would trouble themselves about the survival of the new brand of opera before them or not, and concluding that it didn't matter, implying that such a trivial art-form was not really worthy of extended discussion.[111]

The important point to make about the general reception of *Pirates* is that, as far as George was concerned, he knew that he was a vital part of an exciting new enterprise in the theatre, and he also knew that his colleagues were not only gaining congratulatory reviews, but they were also part of a successful, confident company which was well aware of just how innovative and stimulating was the great partnership of writer and composer they had at the helm.

4

THE SAVOYARD STAR

'It's the song of a merryman, moping mum,
Whose soul was sad and whose glance was glum
Who supped no sup and who craved no sum
As he sighed for the love of a ladye'
W S Gilbert: *The Yeomen of the Guard*

Just as George was on the verge of becoming a key part in the Gilbert and Sullivan enterprise, his idol and inspiration was about to retire from piano entertainment. John Orlando Parry, who George had seen when working with the German-Reeds, had experienced a severe financial crisis and on 7 February 1877 at the Gaiety Theatre, there was a farewell appearance benefit, staged by the manager John Hollingshead. The Prince and Princess of Wales were there, with several aristocrats, and theatre people such as Irving, Corney Grain – and George. Janet Snowman describes the presentation:

> 'For this, his final show, he performed his popular
> pieces, *The Tenor and the Tin Tack*, *The Master and Pupil*
> *or La Lezione do Canto* and *An Operatic Rehearsal! The*
> *Conductor, Tuning, Chorus* etc. along with many of his
> famous songs. These were interwoven with scenes from
> musical plays and dramatic works given by top reformers
> of the day who all came to say farewell and to help him
> out of the financial distress in which he found himself.'[112]

There are many points of interest here with regard to George's career. The first response is that here was a salutary lesson in survival: the great pianist and humorist, in whom George saw the template for his own art, had known the giddy heights and then the deepest falls, of the career they shared. This has to be a reminder that George was always, even in his last days of performance, very much the accountant and manager of his own affairs. He had seen from his father's labours on the road that money was not always forthcoming from the usual

32 Manor Road, Folkestone, where George spent his last years.
(Courtesy of Andrew Hudson)

The Leas at Folkestone, where George was being taken out for the sea air
when he died. *(Courtesy of Andrew Hudson)*

Bow Street Police Court, during the trial of the Fenian bombers in 1867.
George would have been in court, reporting this.
(From The Illustrated London News)

Mr German Reed and Corney Grain, both entertainers and good friends
of George and his circle. *(Courtesy of the Janet Snowman collection)*

B

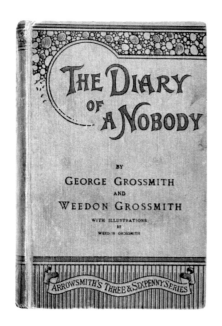

The first edition of *The Diary of a Nobody*, published by Arrowsmiths of Bristol

A pose from the drawings of the original production of *Patience* in 1881

C

A portrait of George at his
most suave and debonair,
ready to entertain.
*(Courtesy of the David
Lovell Collection)*

George Grossmith senior
– 'George the First'.
*(From Gaiety and George
Grossmith, 1913)*

D

George as the jester Jack Point in *The Yeomen of the Guard.*
(Courtesy of the David Lovell Collection)

W S Gilbert.
(Courtesy of Andrew Crowther)

E

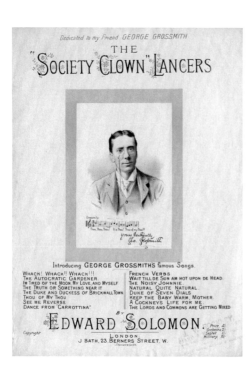

Sheet music for songs by George (top) and GG (below). *(Courtesy of the David Lovell Collection)*

F

Corney Grain, piano entertainer and lawyer. Like George, he had an
interest in the law and in the piano

George's autograph, quoting the famous line from *The Mikado*, which
is arguably most associated with his Gilbert and Sullivan career.
(Courtesy of the David Lovell Collection)

G

George at work as society entertainer. *(From The Daily Graphic, 1890)*

George at home. *(From The Idler magazine, 1897)*

H

MR. JOHN PARRY.

John Parry, the piano entertainer who was a profound influence on George's art and career. *(Courtesy of the Janet Snowman collection)*

George in his famous role of Koko in *The Mikado*.
(Courtesy of the David Lovell Collection)

J

George as the sorcerer John Wellington Wells, his first role for Gilbert and Sullivan. *(Courtesy of the David Lovell Collection)*

K

THE FIRM OF GROSSMITH AND SON.

George and his son GG. *(From Gaiety and George Grossmith, 1913)*

sources; if we add to this the fact that George himself had seen income shrink from the Dolby-organised society parties, and also note that he had kept up the law reporting, then it is clear that by around 1880, even with the new stage career, he was keeping his options open. The reasons for this are easy to find in the social history of the stage in that age of entertainment: principally, there was no security. An injury or serious illness could end a promising career (it has been noted how Jessie Bond carried on working with her open abscess, for instance) and injuries were common in the profession.

Another interesting deduction from other sources uncovered by Janet Snowman is about Parry's performances. In looking at some surviving photographic material held in Wales, it may be concluded that these images, probably from the 1860s at the Gallery of Illustration, and showing Parry with Thomas German-Reed, show a 'knockabout' visual comedy in progress, one picture showing the pair at an easel (Parry was an artist as well as a musician) and the other with a pair of step-ladders, and Parry in female costume. George would have learned from this extension of the basic music-and-patter presentation, that simple situation comedy with minimal props would provide plenty of potential for the mix of verbal and visual comedy he was aiming at. Coincidentally, in my work as an editor for a book on poetry in Liverpool, I once interviewed Roger McGough and he described a similar use of steps with other performers from *The Scaffold* band. McGough explained that it was largely improvised from a basic idea. My impression is that George did more or less the same, with impersonation and gentle satire at the heart of the act.

This period was the point at which music hall was really taking off, and the hall performers also exploited the potential humour of the 'little man in a situation' – this was to become the genre character later taken and embellished by such comics as Dan Leno and Albert Chevalier. There was also George Robey, 'the prime Minister of Mirth' – and all these men had one thing in common, their small stature. George Grossmith had a small, wiry frame. He knew that a small, dapper man would be aligned in the audience's mind with the type of comedy that works on vulnerability and athleticism.

Then there is the factor concerning family life, of course: he had a growing family and a good address to maintain in Marylebone. After 1880, he would also be helping his widowed mother when he could. He had learned independence and the work ethic from his father, and we know from GG that this ethos was carried forward. Yet it is interesting to note here that, according to GG, George was not keen for him to go and tread the boards:

> 'My inborn love of the theatre was frankly not encouraged. My amateur performances, especially those at school, were frowned upon. This was curious, seeing that it was their reputation as brilliant amateurs that had taken my father from journalism and my uncle from portrait painting (to say nothing of my grandfather, great-grandfather and great-great grandfather) to become successful actors and entertainers.'[113]

Around 1880, George was also very much the clubman. Apart from the Savage Club, he was a member of the Beefsteak Club, which had been formed in 1876 by the actor J L Toole, as a reincarnation of the earlier club of that name which had been founded in 1735. The membership was of political, literary and theatrical people, and George's friend Corney Grain was a member, as was Irving, who loved to be active in as many dining clubs as possible. This was arguably all part of that element in the Grossmith dynasty that saw the benefits of freemasonry as well as of networking at dinners, giving talks and so on. Harry Furniss, the artist, wrote an account of the club in his reminiscences:

> 'The Beefsteak Club is the most bohemian club in existence, besides being the most exclusive. It opens at four o'clock in the afternoon, and holds its general meetings at midnight … The members all sit at one large table and everything is arranged to resemble a charming dining room in an old country house. The company are considered to be the best of all the men about town.'[114]

George's social life also extended to that very luxurious and again very sociable pastime, attendance at the Turkish baths. The Savoy Turkish Bath Co was formed in 1883, at Lancaster House, Savoy Street. The secretary was Edmund Bainbridge, and it did very well with theatrical clients, many of whom were also shareholders, including George, along with Francois Cellier, George Edwards and Samuel French. It was a very advanced and modern establishment, with electric lighting, and it was designed by C J Phipps, who was the architect of the newly opened Savoy Theatre. A massive generator powered the theatre's lights and at the first night of *Patience* there, D'Oyly Carte came on stage to smash a bulb and show how safe the new device was. The audience must have recoiled in horror, such was the link between theatres and horrendous fires at the time.

That new theatre was Richard D'Oyly Carte's beloved project; he had planned it for some time, bought the site and raised the finance. In 1881 it was the new location for the comic opera business. Our now familiar term 'the Savoy Operas' originates in that establishment. *Patience*, which had opened at the Opera Comique in 1881, was to be the first opera staged there after being transferred.

After the grand successes of *Pinafore* and *Pirates*, Gilbert turned his satirical eye towards his next target, the theme of 'precious' poetry and the aesthetic movement, seen by the media as the aesthetic trend led by Oscar Wilde which was attracting attention in the press. As one Wilde biographer wrote, 'In 1879 Wilde was still obscure; in 1880 he was famous.'[115] He and his aesthetic friends focused on Wilde's place in Tite Street, and their comings and goings, writings and fashion, became of great media interest. It was at this time that Wilde came to know the painter Whistler, who had at the time created his 'white house' and was extending the imagery of whiteness into art and design. Naturally, such flamboyant characters would attract press attention, and the parodies of their 'art for art's sake' credo began in 1877 when a burlesque called *The Grasshopper* was produced. The targets for parody were Wilde, Whistler and Frank Miles. The next year there was a piece by James Albery. Richard Ellmann, writing of Albery's play *Where's the Cat?* makes it clear that Wilde at first was not enjoying such things, but neither was he bursting with anger and going to his lawyers:

> 'It contained lines like "I feel like – a room without a
> dado" spoken by a character called Scott Ramsay, a writer.
> Herbert Beerbohm Tree played the role with Wilde's
> mannerisms and the play was a success. Wilde made a
> point of not seeing it. At last, three months after the
> opening, Ellen Terry was able to persuade him to share her
> box ... He observed then that the play was poor.'[116]

Wilde's attitude changed when the tide was too strong to turn: a play called *The Colonel* was produced at the Prince of Wales theatre in February 1881, featuring yet another dramatic spoof of Wilde and his well-known habits and poses. It seems almost inevitable, with hindsight, that Gilbert would see the potential for joining the bandwagon and sure enough, the idea for *Patience* was hatched.

At the point at which the opera was going to be presented, and the press knew all about it, Wilde saw the advantages of the 'media PR exercise' and wrote to George, who was to play Bunthorne, the Wilde parodic figure in the piece: 'Dear Grossmith, I should like to go to the first night of your new opera at Easter – and would be very much obliged if you would ask the box office to reserve a three-guinea box for me … With Gilbert and Sullivan I am sure we will have something better than the small farce of *The Colonel*. I am looking forward to being greatly amused.'[117]

A little later, after the success of *Patience*, not only was Wilde amused, but Richard D'Oyly Carte wrote from his New York office to offer Wilde a well-paid lecturing tour around the States, seeing that, as his company were producing *Patience* across the Atlantic, Wilde's tour would be wonderful promotion. Everything went ahead and Wilde had been quite right not to be offended but to join in the fun. Through modern eyes, the satire in *Patience* is very one-dimensional. It has the feel of a joke told at too much length. But in 1881 it has to be recalled just how huge a cultural impact the aesthetic movement was having. Poetry had been, at least in the mainstream highbrow context, very worthy and serious. Major poets were expected, like Tennyson, to provide expression of the great debates, the affirmation of faith after Darwin, and also statements on themes relating to the central social questions of the day. The mid- to late-Victorian years were a period of widespread and popular comic verse in the periodicals and popular press. The comic journals were booming. In the midst of all this, when poetry was related to society and to topical issues and debates, poetry with its own profound lyricism and emotional excess was bound to stir reactions.

This new aestheticism was also a challenge to established masculinity, and it is entirely in keeping with the ideology of male adventure and romance across the Empire that Gilbert chose to have a fine body of men in military garb to set against his aesthetic poets on stage. Again, the pairing of George and Barrington as the two poets (Barrington as Grosvenor) gave the audience their expected laughs from the sight of the tiny, thin George and the very substantial Barrington. George had a great deal more to do in *Patience* than in

Pirates. Therewere some lengthy stretches of song and duets for him to cope with; in some places his skill of shifting from one manner or tone to another was called for, all the while playing up the visual comedy that the public would know from media representations of Wilde and other poets. Essentially, *Patience* is a series of set pieces on infatuation and true love, the familiar Gilbertian playful dialogues. Again, the apparently serious treatment of a farcical theme serves a double purpose: on the surface fun is made from precious, effeminate attitudes to poetry and the specific variety of poet under assault, but in using distorted depictions of the subject, the questionable position of the satirists becomes visible. In other words, the opposition to the kind of attitudes to art being depicted tend to be more extreme than the object of the comedy. This may be seen in the stress on the hollowness and affectation of those who worship the new credo, as in the chorus of maidens, voiced openly by the Lady Angela:

> 'Mystic poet, hear our prayer,
> Twenty love-sick maidens we-
> Young and wealthy, dark and fair-
> All of county family.
> And we die for love of thee
> Twenty love-sick maidens we!'

Put simply, *Patience*, as well as being an unsophisticated attack on Wilde and others, is also a brilliant hatchet-job aimed at the audience which creates the kind of poetry which is adored in the latest artistic vogue.

But there is no doubt that Bunthorne/Wilde is in focus when George has his most protracted scenes, and in the culmination of George's first long scene on his first appearance, Gilbert's central line of attack is clear in the ladies' responses to his song:

ANG. How purely fragrant!
SAPH. How earnestly precious!
PAT. Well it seems to me to be nonsense.
SAPH. Nonsense, yes perhaps – but oh what precious nonsense!'

In one sense, this kind of impersonation – in which George has to act the part of Bunthorne and make all gestures follow the precise direction of the perfectionist, Gilbert – was nothing more than a longer version of his own writing, where social types were lampooned, but there was also much more for him to do in terms of using his body in gestures and balletic movement. He was naturally pushed to the limits, not merely in terms of doing new things, but in the sheer level of emotional intensity involved. He explained in his memoirs that he was a nervous wreck before every performance: 'In taking leave of my readers on the subject of my theatrical career, I feel I ought, in justice to myself, to state that all my first appearances are completely marred by uncontrollable nervousness. I am more than nervous – I am absolutely ill.'[118]

He need not have worried where Bunthorne was concerned. *The Pall Mall Gazette* summed up the theme: 'The unfortunate tendency of human nature to rush into extremes has made the caricaturist in this instance a light one' and then added its delight in the performances: 'The most complete satisfaction may be expressed regarding the performance. Each of the principal characters has an exponent exactly suited to its requirements. Mr Grossmith's make-up as the poet Bunthorne is a study; and equally effective is Mr Rutland Barrington' performance as his rival.'[119] The reviewer for *The Era* had a lot to say on the subject of George's Bunthorne: 'Mr George Grossmith, as the 'fleshly poet', was quite in his element. He invested the character with the grotesque drollery amusing in the extreme and sang the songs with the utmost appreciation of their quaintness', adding that 'The mock dignity of Bunthorne when lording it over the idyllic poet, was also very amusing.'[120] Overall, the feeling one has of the responses to George's Bunthorne is of a certain comic absurdity mixed with the usual grimness and clowning of George and Barrington at their best.

When the production transferred to the new Savoy Theatre, in the inevitable maelstrom of excitement and expectancy, George was especially favoured, as the leading man, being given a dressing room to himself. It must have been a time of immense elation, yet for George it was a first night he was destined to miss. His mother died on 27 February after a long illness. As Tony Joseph has pointed out, Louisa Grossmith is a 'shadowy figure' in the Grossmith story. We have glimpses of her, as when GG recalled her having evenings with Theosophists or scientists, and the visits to see George at work: GG wrote about two lady playgoers and his own family, that 'No visitors was I happier or prouder to welcome than my own family and for none did Miss Foster and Harding make more majestic preparation. These visits were not frequent – only a little more frequent than the wondrous visits we children made with our mother to the Savoy to have tea with "The Lord Chancellor," "Ko-Ko" or "Jack Point."[121]

George now moved on to play the usual lead male part in the next Savoy production, *Iolanthe*. Gilbert's love of exploiting 'Fairyland' in a 'topsy-turvy world' surfaced again here: in one of his *Bab Ballads*, 'The Fairy Curate' had been the first expression of the basic story in *Iolanthe*. The theme is the marriage of a curate and a fairy, with the resultant fun and hi-jinks, as in this account of their son, Georgie:

> *'Time progressing,*
> *Georgie's blessing*
> *Grew more ritualistic -*
> *Popish scandals,*
> *Tonsures, sandals -'*

But in *Iolanthe* there was also the introduction of one of George's most successful roles – that of the Lord Chancellor. As with the Major General and Wolseley, there was a model from real life here, in Lord Lyndhurst, a man with a reputation admirably summed up by Robert Blake:

> '... although Lyndhurst was a man of brilliant parts and considerable legal ability, he did not inspire trust. The licence of his conversation, his ribaldry and cynicism, his general levity of demeanour were ill calculated to give him a reputation for seriousness of purpose.'[122]

Blake added to this the point that 'He was a notorious pursuer of women ... Lyndhurst's conversation was reckless in the extreme.'[123]

Not only had Lyndhurst, who died in 1863, been Lord Chancellor three times, he was the man who had, in 1835, seen an act through parliament which failed to remedy the ongoing statute forbidding a man's marriage with his deceased wife's sister. Just a few years before *Iolanthe* was produced, there had been a long debate and a prolonged second reading of a bill to change these matters and to prevent such couples having to go abroad to marry. This was to be debated for a long time yet – finally being passed in 1907 as the Deceased Wife's Sister Marriage Act.

Iolanthe is very much about marriage – as is so often the case with Gilbert's work – and not only does the play take a swipe at the prohibition of such marriages, in the lines spoken by the Fairy Queen, '*He shall prick that annual blister/marriage with deceased wife's sister,*' but it has a laugh at an even more ridiculous situation: the love of a Lord for one of his wards of Chancery. Basically, Gilbert explores various dilemmas of affection and betrothal, and one feels sure that the audience in 1882 were fully aware of the shadow of the Lyndhurst Act over the show.

In 1879 at the second reading of the bill, the Prince of Wales had started the proceedings, and he said, 'It is my firm conviction that if this Bill passed it would be of advantage to the community at large; and I shall, therefore, give my hearty support to the noble Lord who moves the second reading ...'[124] The Lord in question was Lord Houghton, and he reminded everyone of the 1835 Act of the Chancellor: 'There neither was, nor is there, in fact, in the Statute Book of any country in the world an Act so inconsistent in its provisions, so repugnant to common sense, and so shocking in the first dictates of morality... notwithstanding the passing of Lord Lyndhurst's Act, virtuous men and women went on contracting these marriages...'[125] In the end, the Contents were defeated by the Not Contents by 101/81. The House of Lords was to blame for the subject going on yet again, unresolved. This was in spite of several petitions, such as one from the farmers of Norfolk (3,258 of them) who were praying for the legalisation of marriage with a deceased wife's sister.

Hence, in *Iolanthe,* the Lords are under assault by the satirist as well as the absurdities of the marriage legality laws. All this social and legal history lies behind the songs and patters of George as he presents the Lord Chancellor to the audience, who were well aware of the 'law's delay' in this matter. With each opera after *Pirates*, Gilbert's writing and themes tended to shift focus from one central target if there was no easily identifiable satirical strain in the overall plot; hence in *Patience* there were the aesthetes, and no real dissipation of themes. Then, in *Iolanthe* and more so in *Princess Ida*, the tight line of satire is not always held, with an indulgence in labouring some of the ideas in lengthy scenes. But as far as George was concerned, his parts in these two pieces (preceding the real triumph and return to form of Gilbert, as some would argue, in *The Mikado*), were still very much his cup of tea, with a range of commentary, beginning with his song 'The law is a true embodiment' which has the basis of the humour in his lines

'But there'd be the deuce to pay in the Lords/ If I fell in love with one of my wards' and building to the famous dream song, 'While you're lying awake.' Yet it is in the song in Act 1 'When I went to the Bar as a very young man' that had a strong resonance with the public in the early 80s: the lines there, expressing the abuse of the judge's power in the courts, run through the potential errors and failures within the use of the professional powers of the highest men in the legal profession. After all, this was a time in which a judge in his court was a mighty potentate, and his work was very highly paid. When we reflect on the potency of the judge's directions to the jury at that time, and his potential to bias the interpretation of a case, Gilbert's words really hit home. Such lines as 'Ere I go into court I will read my brief through ... and I'll never take work I'm unable to do' were perfectly expressed for George to exercise his creative control of end-rhymes, switching from speech to song, and using the force of emphasis and irony to give the song the utmost effect.

In the 'dream' song Gilbert infuses the piece with the vigour of his best Bab Ballads, creating in effect a monologue with a 'storyboard' of images for the actor to follow, starting with a description of the tormented lover unable to sleep, and launching into a surreal, overstretched story that can be a mix of a series of mimes as in a tableau, with a 'commentary' in the patter, and this effect is strengthened by the use of internal rhymes in long lines, as in:

> 'But this you can't stand, so you throw up your hand
> And you find you're as cold as an icicle,
> In your shirt and your socks (the black silk with gold clocks)
> Crossing Salisbury Plain on a bicycle'

Clearly, George was adept at varying the pace of his delivery, so that the machinegun speed of some lines or part-lines is counteracted by the changes of pace when the meaning dictates it.

The ultimate pastiche on the status and attitudes of the Lord Chancellor comes when everything has to be put right after the 'misprisons' as Shakespeare would have called them, are disclosed: 'Allow me, as an old equity draughtsman, to make a suggestion. The subtleties of the legal mind are equal to the emergency. The thing is really quite simple ... Let it stand that every fairy shall die who don't marry a mortal, and there you are, out of your difficulty at once!'

As usual with a Savoy opera, the impact on the audiences at the time of the first productions is wonderfully multivalent and complex:

as they laughed at the resolution of the burletta-type ridiculous 'fairyland' plot, there was the undertone of reference to the law in the real world. Defendants in trials, criminal and civil, were in the hands of an authoritarian, professional law machine, with a rigidity in procedure which could be formidable and terrifying. In the case of criminal trials, defendants could not speak for themselves until there were changes in the use and presentation of evidence in the mid-1890s; when that reform did occur in 1896, allowing the accused to enter the witness box, the great judge Lord Brampton wrote that 'It must be apparent to everyone, learned and unlearned in its mysteries, that no evidence can be of its highest value ... until sifted by cross-examination.' That is, the legal profession feared that defendants would suffer and should be kept silent.[126]

The law, beneath all the fun and the irony in *Iolanthe,* was a great edifice, generating fear and confusion. Satire has to poke fun at everything of course; nothing is sacred, and Gilbert realised, as he had done in *Trial by Jury* earlier in his career, that there was considerable humour in the wig and gown, the style and dash of barristers. He made his topsy-turvy story enjoyable, with George given the main responsibility of imbuing the Lord Chancellor with a personality all would take to and laugh *at* as well as *with*.

Princess Ida was rather a different matter. It was produced at the Savoy on 5 January 1884. Henry Spencer Ashbee, theatregoer, writer and possible author of the erotic classic, *My Secret Life* by 'Walter', located the weakness in his diary note, while at the same time summing up George's virtues and failings:

> 'February 14 1884. Took Elizabeth and Frances to the Savoy Theatre to see the Princess Ida, by far the weakest comic opera of Gilbert and Sullivan which has yet appeared. Much more might have been made out of the Princess, and of the music, scarcely a bar struck me as original. Barrington's part did not suit him. The same may be said of Miss Braham. Grossmith was as usual admirable, in spite of his want of voice, but he had not enough to do. The mise en scene as usual most beautiful.'[127]

Ashbee is quite right: Grossmith as King Gama was not on stage for the whole of the second act, in this three-act piece (the only one in the Savoy operas). Visually, his part was compelling, being somewhere between the worst melodramatic representations of Shakespeare's Richard III and a puny weakling of very unregal stature. In fact, looking at the drawings of George as King Gama, one striking similarity comes to mind: the figure of the king in a burlesque, *Bombastes Furioso,* by William Barnes Rhodes, first printed in 1810 but reprinted in 1873 with drawings by George Cruikshank. But basically, Richard III comes through, as he had been played innumerable times in the fifty years before *Princess Ida*.[128] There were many factors stacked against the opera's success, not the least being that it was a spoof of Tennyson's poem *The Princess*. As Derek Hudson has pointed out, the responses were not encouraging: 'The newspaper criticisms were mixed; the word "dull" appeared in several of them.'[129] In these lines from Tennyson's poem we have the germ of the idea which had attracted Gilbert:

'Quick answered Lilia, "There are thousands now.
Such women, but convention beats them down...
...Oh I wish
That I were some great princess, I would build
Far off from men a college like a man's,
And I would teach tem all that men are taught;
We are twice as quick!" And here she shook aside
The hand that played the patron with her curls.'[130]

The writing and musical settings for *Princess Ida* were a watershed in the trajectory of the highly successful partnership of Gilbert and Sullivan. The latter was desperately ill with a recurrent kidney ailment, and had forced himself to keep a commission for the Leeds Music Festival as well as taking on the new Savoy work. There was also a deeper problem for Sullivan, who was a very gifted composer in a variety of classical genres with a solid background in serious musical studies. Basically, the triviality of the comic operas was wearing him down, with a mix of aesthetic disappointment and frustration at the operas generally. He complained about these problems in a letter to Gilbert which marked their first quarrel: 'I will be frank. With *Princess Ida* I have come to the end of my tether – the end of my capability in that class of piece. My tunes are in danger of becoming repetitions of my former pieces ...' Then he added, 'I should like to set a story of human interest and probability ... There would then be a feeling of reality about it which would give fresh interest in writing.'[131]

The press were aware of the quarrel, and in *The Star* one report was revelling in the news: 'It is quite true about the Gilbert and Sullivan split. The two kings of Barataria are at such odds that they actually do not speak to one another … They have been linked together with a closeness that makes the association of Damon and Pythias a mere casual friendship by comparison … In so long and so close an association there must have been many little differences…'[132]

Clearly, it was a problem with the genre and with the dissatisfaction of giving the public more of the same. This came after Sullivan had made a gargantuan effort on the first night of the opera, managing to see the performance to the end before collapsing. He was ordered to rest for a long period, and to avoid any extreme activity. That period of sickness and recuperation had given him pause: naturally he had taken a long look at his career and saw that his skills were being wasted. What made matters worse for D'Oyly Carte and Sullivan was that *Princess Ida* was not a success, and by the early autumn it was clear that it marked a falling off, with some vital element missing. George as King Gama and Rutland Barrington as King Hildebrand had been assigned roles which left a lot to be desired, the parts not extending them, nor offering something that used their comic abilities.

Princess Ida does have stretches of what could politely be called less-than-excellent dramatic interest: the setting is the usual imaginary quasi-neverland and the plot is basically summed up in Hildebrand's lines:

> '…. *If Gama fail*
> *To put in an appearance at our court*
> *Before the sun has set in yonder west,*
> *And fail to bring the Princess Ida here*
> *To whom our son Hilarion was betrothed*
> *At the extremely early age of one,*
> *There's war between King Gama and ourselves.*[133]

What emerges is mainly a ridiculous boss-eyed view of 'bluestockings' and the proto-versions of the 'New Woman' of the time. But in the crazy core of all this, George as Gama does at least have one classically tuneful and dynamic song which has found a place in the canon of Gilbert and Sullivan's 'hits.' This is 'If you give me your attention, I will tell you what I am' with the refrains in each stanza of *'Yet everybody says I'm such a disagreeable man! /And I can't think why!'* George played it with his usual aplomb and the lines cry out for his own inimitable style of delivery, with a strong expression of nastiness to match the best villains of melodrama.

However, the piece as a whole disappointed. As Andrew Crowther has put it, 'It was spectacular and entertaining but there was something missing … Carte wrote to the two collaborators giving them their six months' notice for the creation of a new opera.'[134] There is no doubt that Gilbert had his finger on the pulse with regard to the importance of a 'college for women' because during the time he wrote *Princess Ida*, there had been a meeting at the Mansion House supporting plans for King's College to extend their courses to women students; then there was the College for Working Women, providing evening classes at Fitzroy Street, and in July 1884, as *Ida* was playing to the dwindling audiences, there was much discussion of the opening of Alexandra House as part of the Home for Lady Art Students in Brunswick Square, and Queen Victoria's daughter, Princess Louise, Duchess of Argyll, was a talented artist and sculptor. Gilbert saw the topicality in his theme, as usual, but there was a decline in the appeal and nothing could be done to put it right.

It must have seemed as though the magical, creative duo had reached their end. But then, the story is that Gilbert was in his library when he saw a large Japanese sword fall from the wall. As he picked it up, thoughts relating to the current fad for things Japanese came into his head, and he decided to focus on a story with a Japanese setting. From the mid-1880s there were several factors that put Japanese art and culture prominently before the public, most prominently the Japanese Exhibition at Knightsbridge where a Japanese 'village' had been set up. This would lead to such cultural events as the founding of the Japan Society in 1891 and to Japanese artistry working its way into popular furnishing and décor.

What Gilbert was to do played a major part in this acceleration of the Japanese fever in artistic matters: he had formed the genesis of what was to be *The Mikado*. When he told Sullivan of his idea, the response was more than encouraging: 'If I understand you to propose you will construct a plot without the supernatural and improbable elements … I gladly undertake to set it without further discussing the matter, or asking what the subject to be.'[135] This new concord was more than welcome, not least because if Sullivan had withdrawn from the Savoy enterprise, the contract between the two creative minds and the management would have been broken.

During all this, in the early- to mid-80s, George was busy with the Savoy work, but also carried on with other engagements. Wherever there was a soirée, a benefit concert or any kind of occasion at which his ever-widening circle of friends needed him, he and his piano were there. Emily Soldene, the actress, was trying her hand at management, and she gives us a glimpse into a typical such party, in this case given by Mrs and Mrs Head, for the twenty-first birthday of their son. Her memory also tells us a lot about the close friendship of George and the great actor Henry Irving:

> 'Among the company was a distinguished-looking
> gentleman, of A most delightful and affable turn, who
> would do anything to amuse or oblige. Just when I
> arrived, he was giving a recitation… with a mannerism
> I much admired. "Who is it?" said I to a friend. "Don't
> you know?" said he. I shook my head. After a few
> minutes our host brought the gentleman up: "Let me
> introduce Mr Irving." There was also another bright and
> entertaining luminary present, Mr George Grossmith,
> who gave us a sketch from his penny Readings and sang,
> "I am so Volatile." Lots of professional people were among
> the guests: Mr D'Oyly Carte, Mr J L Toole, Fred and
> Harry Payne … we were a very merry and representative
> crowd.'[136]

In 1885, on the eve of the opening night of *The Mikado*, George Grossmith was indeed a 'luminary' as Emily put it. The scenes we find him in recall the same conviviality as his father, and the same desire for companionship, along with his irresistible drive to entertain and keep everyone amused. He was the one you asked if you wanted to ensure that all went smoothly at any kind of gathering. Here was a man of almost forty, with a young family and a life so busy that he must never have known an instant of boredom; he was writing, performing, being a celebrity (often rather reluctantly so) and finding time to be a father and husband. In 1885 GG was eleven: Lawrence and Cordelia were too young to aspire as yet to any notable part in the endless pastimes, sports and singing that filled the home in Dorset Square. GG was still a long way from thinking of the theatre, as he notes at the opening of his autobiography: 'I had no thought of the stage until at eighteen years of age my father informed me one morning that the late W S Gilbert had invited me to make my debut in his new opera, for which my father was providing the score.'[137]

There is no doubt, in spite of the small space George allows in his memoirs to talk about his home life, that the Grossmith family were happy and fulfilled: as with George the First, George's view of family happiness was perhaps the same as Thomas Gray's: 'To be happy is to be perpetually employed.' For the Grossmith angle on life, business meant busyness. He was certainly going to be busy as *The Mikado* was in the process of being rehearsed and then launched on a public who were expecting the famous duo to produce the goods this time.

There was a little drama, also, in the space between the demise of *Princess Ida* and the arrival of *The Mikado*. As *Princess Ida* faded away, and *The Sorcerer* revival was hastily put in place, with George returning to his character of John Wellington Wells, he and Barrington made the newspapers for a reason entirely unconnected to the comic opera: they were seriously ill. *The Era* reported this:

> 'Mr George Grossmith and Mr Rutland Barrington
> have been poisoned by oysters. They partook of a few
> 'natives' for luncheon after rehearsal last Thursday week
> … and the next morning both were seized with cholerine.
> Mr Grossmith, who was at Datchet at the time, was so
> seriously indisposed that he could not play at the Savoy
> Theatre either Friday or Saturday …'[138]

When he recovered he saw out the re-run of *The Sorcerer*: meanwhile *The Mikado* was moving towards completion. The role of Ko-Ko the Lord High Executioner, was arguably to be George's best role, in the sense that he had to play in the midst of a bundle of confusing paradoxes, as witty as Gilbert had ever been before in his writing, with quick-fire humour across a range of styles and manners. As Barrington played Pooh-Ba, Lord High Everything Else, their interchanges must have sparkled, as so much of the muddlement relies on jokes about execution, suicide and strange twists of legal rulings which (as so often with Gilbert) were mercilessly ridiculed. Yet in addition to this, there are some scenes in which the audience would have seen as commentary on the current criminal law, as in the scene with Ko-Ko and Pitti-Sing in Act II with this passage:

'The criminal cried, as he dropped him down,
In a state of wild alarm –
With a frightful, frantic, fearful frown,
I bared my big right arm.
I seized him by his little pig-tail
And on his knees fell he…'

There would have been many in the audience who had seen public executions, which had not ended until 1868; but any such echoes of reality were rescued and dipped into the realms of the absurd, as in Gilbert's exquisite use of bathos, such as in these lines after giving a death sentence: 'I forget the punishment for compassing the death of the heir apparent … Something lingering, with boiling oil in it, I fancy. Something of that sort. I think boiling oil occurs in it but I'm not sure.'

George was in his element, having rapid, witty repartee with a dash of the surreal to enjoy, as in his weeping after confessing that he has no experience of killing people, and lamenting that he would not have accepted the post of Lord High Executioner had he known it was not 'purely nominal.' Then of course, he has some marvellous songs, including 'As some day it may happen …' with its dynamic refrain of *'I've got them on the list/They'd none of 'em be missed.'*

But the first night was horrific for him. George went to pieces, forgetting lines and being out of kilter with everything around him. The root of this was in George's nerves; he explains in *A Society Clown* that this problem was always with him: 'all my first appearances are completely marred by uncontrollable nervousness', he wrote. He then adds his own version of the mess he made of *The Mikado*:

'The first night of The Mikado I shall never forget the longest day I live. It must have appeared to all that I was doing my best to spoil the piece. But what with my own want of physical strength, prostration through the numerous and very long rehearsals, my anxiety to satisfy the author, the rows of critics (oh please do not be hard on me!) rendered blasé by the modern custom of half a dozen and senseless matinees a week, I lose my voice the little there is of it, my confidence, and what I maintain is most valuable to me, my own individuality.'[139]

70

Sullivan, in his diary, was not too upset, merely writing that all went well 'except Grossmith whose nervousness nearly upset the piece.'[140] But on the credit side for George at this time was that it took very little to redeem himself, such was his popularity, and a review in *Punch* described what he did: 'Suddenly in the second act he gave a kick-up, and showed a pair of white-stockinged legs under the Japanese dress. It was an inspiration. Forthwith the house felt a strong sense of relief …'[141]

Gilbert's efforts to research costume properly paid off; he had a Japanese woman help with the research, even to the extent of having her teach the cast how to use fans. It was not too difficult to see Japanese costume: there was not only a current exhibition on the nation and its culture, but a Japanese village set up in Knightsbridge. George's costume was very striking, and one of the classic Gilbert and Sullivan images is that of George as Ko-Ko, eyes half closed, wearing a beautiful coat decorated with dragons and storks. Some of the costumes used were possessions of people who let their heirlooms be borrowed, rather than the company having to have all the costumes specially made.[142]

If we pause at this point, to reflect on George's career with Gilbert and Sullivan, what emerges most prominently is his acquisition of all the essential elements of the image of a showman at the time: he was a Savoy celebrity, piano man and socialite – in modern parlance, an artist with quite a portfolio. That he should have achieved the leap from a comic on the fringe of music hall and soirée performance to artist on tour (with the Pauls and with Florence Marryat) then again, that he was able to transform all that into a major London star, is stunningly impressive. The secret of success lies primarily in his image: here was a man who was wiry, rather frail-looking, but infinitely adaptable in the sense of being able to tackle a wide range of comic roles. Above all that there was his sparkling wit and unerring sense of comic pause and delivery of lines. Before working for the Savoy management, he had stepped up from solo pianist to one of an ensemble, and he had also proved himself as a writer, having found his natural genre in that respect – short dramas, tailor-made to be prologues to main attractions or for use in cabaret and small-scale occasions. He had learned to write comedy which needed few props or any elaborate staging; he was thoroughly at home in dialogue, and could infuse the most mundane conversation with something surprising or laughable.

What must have attracted him – and Gilbert knew this – were roles in which he could be an entertainer. So his last role for Gilbert and Sullivan was to be that of Jack Point, 'a strolling jester' but first he had one more challenging part, the dual character of Murgatroyd/ Oakapple in *Ruddigore*. There was a dark cloud over the *Ruddigore* part, though, as George fell seriously ill.

The opera did not start well: Derek Hudson summed up the problem: '*Ruddigore* never perhaps wholly emerged from its disappointing initial reception … the blend of gay and grotesque did not make an entirely satisfactory whole.'[143] Reading the text, aside from looking at any actual performance, there is a sense of a slackening of the humour of previous operas, in spite of some very successful comic moments. Once again, the theme concerns marriage and also punishment, along with more perspectives on crime from Gilbert the lawyer of course. It has one of his more successful playful concepts – that the Barons Murgatroyd have to commit a crime a day or, as the witch's curse which was the origin of this stated, 'In torture he shall die!'

The result is plenty of the usual Savoy baloney with surreal situations, and George had some of the best, such as the lively 'My boy you may take it from me' with its deliciously slangy lines: *'You must stir it and stump it/ and blow your own trumpet.'* The reviews were positive: 'Mr George Grossmith, in the character of Robin, has a part rather out of the usual line – but which he plays with his customary tact and ability' in *The Musical Times*, and 'He was seldom off the stage and whatever he did when on it was done with every help from an artistic nature and consummate skill' in *The Daily Telegraph*.[144] 'Playgoer' of *The Penny Illustrated Paper* gave it a long feature on the first night, with a summary of the plot, beginning the review with a focus on George and noting that one had to 'shut ones eyes' to register the fact that one was seeing 'George Grossmith as a retiring village swain.'[145]

But just a week or so into the production, George was smitten by a serious and life-threatening illness – peritonitis. He collapsed, and was confined to bed rest. Some papers simply had the line 'Mr George Grossmith is seriously ill at his house in Dorset Square.' Not much was reported, but we know that one of the best medical men in the land attended him – Edward Sieveking, who was to be knighted by the Queen less than a year later (which shows what social connections George had). The Prince of Wales sent his best wishes to George, as well as the doctor, and of course, the Prince and his wife had been entertained by George in earlier times, at society parties. Sieveking was a very talented and forward-looking man; he was involved in nurse training and had a special interest in neurology. George was ill for over two weeks, and went to Brighton when the worst was over, for recuperation.

During George's illness, Henry Lytton stepped in to take the part, and so the next comic star had his first chance in the limelight. As Leslie Baily commented, 'The audience was disappointed and chilling when it found an unknown stripling in the part of Robin Oakapple but the charm of Lytton won them over …'[146] Then, when George recovered, he learned how truly loved he was by his public: Tony Joseph points out that George received 'a flood of telegrams and letters of sympathy and anxious good wishes.'[147]

But work soon resumed, and the press announced that George would be back, appearing every night and on Saturday afternoons, in *Ruddigore*. We can measure the extent of his recovery and return to form by the fact that, just six weeks later, he was appearing in a burlesque of the opera at Toole's theatre, entitled *Ruddy George*. His close friend, J L Toole, written by G F Taylor and Percy Reeves had organised this, purely for fun. In George's life and thespian circles, nothing was above being the target of fun and games, and the current hit was no exception. *The Era* reported, with a sense of playfulness, 'Though a burlesque on Ruddigore is an impossibility, there was room for some good natured pleasantry' and the writer mentions something not often commented on in George's life: 'Mr George Grossmith, in a sketch several times done by him, called The Drama on Crutches, used to give an exceedingly droll skit on the Savoy operas.'[148] Obviously, Rutland Barrington, who was part of the fun, had a laugh at his friend: 'There was an attempt to twit Mr Grossmith with his thin voice and his invariable knowledge of his part … there seemed to be an intention, too, to ridicule Mr Barrington's vocal peculiarities …'[149] The whole party of players were having fun at each other's expense, mercilessly satirising themselves.

J L Toole was a very good friend; they were so close that they shared boyish jokes and tricks, and both were always keen to let loose their love of ridicule and parody. As Frank Archer wrote, Toole was 'essentially a farce actor' and he added in his memoir of working with Toole that, 'His personal home trials had been very severe for he outlived wife and children and there was unusual sadness in his last days of suffering … Thousands of his good deeds were, I know, unchronicled in any record.'[150] Toole died in Brighton in July 1906. His autobiography contains plenty of information on George, and it is arguably in Toole that George found the actor who had the sense of humour and general view of life that was closest to his own.

Typical of George also was the fact that he still maintained his diary, so that we know that in between Savoy performances, he was at the piano, and writing new material. Around this time he appears to have written and performed what became his most well-known song, mentioned in one report of his appearance at Colchester, in a musical matinee at the Drill Hall in April:

> 'The star of the programme was of course Mr Grossmith, who has never produced a more amusing sketch then the one he gave, entitled "Homburg." It is impossible in print to describe the piece. In it he relates in that droll and very amusing fashion, which is his alone, how he spent a month at Homburg in the hope of getting away from English associations in general, and Mikado associations in particular, and his ludicrous account of the way in which these associations turned up wherever he went created much laughter. The very witty songs and clever musical introductions… rendered the sketch one of his chefs d'oeuvres.. and the audience required his reappearance … Mr Grossmith responded by singing an exceedingly laughable and clever song … See Me Dance the Polka …'[151]

The subject of Homburg was particularly topical. It was one of the favourite leisure spots of the Prince of Wales, and papers reported unfavourably on his habits there, notably his gambling.[152] Homburg was a spa town, famous for its hat manufacture, the hat being made popular by the Prince. So there was plenty of contemporary reference for George to use.

As *Ruddigore* was stopped earlier than was usual at the Savoy, in November 1887, there was yet again a sense of disappointment and frustration in Gilbert and Sullivan's relationship. Sullivan had been drafting out his next opera, something set in the Tower of London, and he was pleased with it. Once again, he had George in mind for a key role, and it was to be his last – Jack Point, the strolling player. In contrast to *Ruddigore*, it was to be very well received.

The Yeomen of the Guard opened on 3 October 1888. George's last great starring role for the duo, who were by that time national institutions, was peculiarly fitting for his personality and with regard to his professional life. Jack Point has a lot to do, from the first line of the chorus in Act I which has, *'Here's a man of jollity/ Jibe, joke, jollify!'* the emphasis is on humour, with George's very first little piece of speech containing the homely wisdom of: 'For look you, there is humour in all things, and the truest philosophy is that which teaches us to make the most of it.' For the character, Gilbert relied heavily on Shakespearean clowns, notably Jacques and Touchstone, providing in Jack Point the jokes along with the rather laboured kind of puns and double-talk that the Elizabethans clearly enjoyed.

As the plot concerns the ruse of the prisoner Fairfax escaping the axe, and for reasons of law and inheritance, his marrying Elsie (beloved of Jack, his strolling player mate), then Jack is ultimately left alone, and so built into the part of Jack is another thread. This relates to Shakespearean fools, with their isolation, their destiny to be alone and separate from the lovers in the plays, as for instance Touchstone is at the end of *As You Like It,* when all the other characters pair up and dance. Gilbert was obviously influenced by this, and it seems that he wanted a similarly sad ending. In George's case, his last lines in the opera, in his part in the duet with Elsie, are:

> *Heighdy! Heighdy!*
> *Misery me, lackadaydee!*
> *He sipped no sup and he craved no crumb*
> *For he lived in the love of a ladye!'*

George never did this with much more than another cause for a laugh, in spite of the preceding lines being *'It's the song of a merryman, moping mum/ whose soul was sad and whose glance was glum/ as he sighed for the love of a lady.'* Many years from then, in the 1922 obituary of George Thorne, an actor who took over Grossmith's role, was this comment, in a heading proclaiming him as 'The man who gave jack Point a tragic end': 'He was an ideal Savoyard, a comedian of rare artistry, and with a sense of the pathetic, which made him give the part of Jack Point, which Mr George Grossmith had always played for a laugh, a tragic end.'[153] Arguably, as the character of Jack Point is in the Elizabethan tradition, the melancholy strain in the character has to accept loss and misery as part of life, and even make jokes from it. That was the basis of George's interpretation, and of course it has to be recalled that Gilbert always directed closely and insisted on his lines being delivered in a specific way. But there is the undisputed sadness at the end, because the stage direction is 'Fairfax embraces Elsie as Point falls insensible at their feet.'

However, there is no denying that George as Jack has wonderful humour to use, the highlight being 'Oh a private buffoon is a light-hearted loon.' But he also has more dialogue than usual, solely devoted to the discussion and practice of a variety of verbal wit. It is easy to imagine George working the audience with this, making the most of all the weak jokes, employing his established mix of movement and intonation. Yet the debate on what he did to the role lumbered on. Tony Joseph sums up the heart of the issue:

> 'But in later years the idea gained currency that he had not so much toned down the tragedy as turned it into clownish comedy ... He fell down in a way that was 'irresistibly funny [Henry Lytton's words]; while a story even circulated that as the curtain fell on the first night, the "insensible" jester, lying prostrate in the centre of the stage, raised a leg and waggled it playfully...'[154]

It was the end of George's main participation in the Savoy enterprise. He was so popular across the land that he was turning down offers of work all the time. He was missing what he perhaps enjoyed more than any other aspect of his professional life: entertaining an audience with variety – his mix of humour and song, and performing his own work, rather than delivering someone else's lines. Early in 1889 he told the Savoy management that he was leaving the company. Gilbert, wanting to keep him in the fold, wrote to Sullivan about George and in that letter we have a candid assessment: 'Don't you think we ought to mark Grossmith's departure by a present of some kind? He is a d....d bad actor, but he has worked very hard for us.'[155] This sounds very much like a back-handed compliment, and it is in keeping with the man's character.

George had indeed worked hard. As Gilbert told an interviewer in 1890:

'Just now Mr Grossmith is taking much pleasure in doing the round of the theatres. I quoted the old saying about actors' holidays. "But you forget," he replied, " that for the twelve years I was at the Savoy I had scarcely any chance of sitting before the curtain. There was a succession of long runs and no vacations.'[156]

He was never the one for excess in expressing any personal reflection, and in *A Society Clown* all he devotes to that leaving is one short paragraph: 'In concluding this chapter, let me offer my hearty thanks to Sir Arthur Sullivan for having thought of me, to D'Oyly Carte for having engaged me, and last but not least to the generous public for having tolerated me.'[157]

George did eventually receive his farewell gift from Gilbert and Sullivan, in the shape of two silver punch bowls with this inscription:

To George Grossmith
from Arthur Sullivan, W S Gilbert
and R D'Oyly Carte,
at the close of his first
theatrical engagement,
which lasted twelve years
1877-1889

5

PIANO MAN

'Give me a laundry-list and I'll set it to music'
(reputedly) said by Gioacchino Rossini

George was at the piano again for the coming years, apart from occasional work in Savoy revivals. He was to become a strolling player like Jack Point, and his diary was destined to be full. Life was to be a succession of dates, appointments, performances and hasty notes and letters, just as was the case with his friend's life, his old colleague Corney Grain. We have a glimpse of this in a letter written by Corney from the Beefsteak Club in May 1889 to a Mrs Robertson, in which he wrote: 'I could come February 15 (Saturday) 1890. Would the train due at Broxbourne at 7.36 p.m. do? It would give me time to get something to eat after my work.'[158] It is clear from this that the travelling piano man had to keep control of his diary and itinerary. Of course, that life had never really stopped. Tony Joseph, in his biography of Grossmith, lists a sample number of engagements between 1884 and 1888 and these include only London addresses, but he rarely missed a chance to take part in a benefit or a charity fundraising appearance.

George was about to resume his life of society entertainer, and he was in charge of his own diary, and also of his own way of doing things. There is no doubt that Gilbert had been a hard taskmaster; a workhorse absolutely dedicated to writing and producing in his way. Now George was no longer subject to the Savoy regime nor Gilbert's methods, described by Michael Kilgarriff: 'Before rehearsals started he would work out every move with the aid of a model stage; all exits and entrances, gestures, dances and even make-up were minutely regulated and he brooked no diversions from his instructions.'[159] Being interviewed by critic William Archer in 1903 Gilbert said, 'I knew exactly what groupings I wanted – how many people I could have on this bank, how many on that rostrum and so forth. I had it all clear in my head before going down to the theatre and there the actors and actresses were good enough to believe in me and to lend themselves heartily to all I required of them.'[160]

Now George was master of his own fate. Reading between the lines, we can see that such restraints and rules would not be matters easily accommodated into George's way of performing, although of course he was a great success in the regime.

He was also going solo again at a time when music hall had enjoyed its first main flowering and there was a certain dispersal of musical and comedy entertainers into distinct types who catered for different audiences. Peter Bailey has researched the place of society entertainers in this development, and we can see where George fits in here:

'The social significance of these trends lay in the fact that society entertainers and sketch artistes cultivated an air of middle class refinement rather alien to music hall circles. Theatrical sketch artistes reminded 'pros' of the great social gulf between halls and the legitimate theatre … Society entertainers were traditionally associated with drawing room, salon and concert hall venues, and they basked in the reflected glory of their superior patrons and audiences.'[161]

George was a type of 'sketch artist' but in the higher reaches of that group. He certainly had the high-class patrons and appearances, including royalty and aristocracy. His special blend of articulate and allusive song and sketch may be attributed to the literary basis of his attitudes and tastes, with George the First visible there in the range of influences behind his art.

This is the ideal point to look at the roots of George's variety of piano entertainment, and Harold Scott's account of the genre, written in 1946, is very helpful here. Mention has already been made of John Parry and of course, Corney Grain, who introduced George to the society work, but behind them all, as Scott explained, was Charles Dibdin, whose influence 'is directly traceable in many of the entertainments of the 1850s, notably in those of Albert Smith and John Orlando Parry.'[162] Dibdin's work in the genre goes back to 1788 when he devised what he called a musical lecture or 'soirée, and he called it *The Whim of the Moment*. Scott described Dibdin's art in this way:

'The genius of this extraordinary man was here fully exploited, for he possessed versatile talents as an actor, composer, singer and author. It is said that few of his songs took him more than half an hour to compose. He had the same felicity with lyrics and dialogue, which he presented in an easy naturalness of style described as ' that of a person entertaining a party of friends in a drawing room …'[163]

Those words could apply to George. People who saw Dibdin commented on his way of being happy and expressing joy and whimsicality from the instant of his entrance, and accounts of George's act give the same impression. He had seen Parry, and of course he knew that Parry (as also was the case with Dibdin) was also an artist and used that skill at times in his act. George's focus was on what he did best: humorous lyrics and comedic movement.

He understood the range and variety of his various audiences, and in *A Society Clown* he described the features of the different events at different times. One striking aspect of his entertainments was the enterprise he had in trying new things. One outstanding example of this is his providing a skit on Sheridan's *The School for Scandal* at the home of John Aird in Hyde Park Terrace. Aird was an MP and head of the great firm of engineers which he had taken over from his father in 1870. His Gas Light and Coke Company fuelled all of London north of the Thames by 1875. As his biographer explained, he even had a private theatre 'to which plays were brought to him to save the journey and inconvenience of going to the theatre … Almost meticulous in pursuit of the grand manner he would at his dinner parties present every woman with a gift … Always he loved to be at the centre of parties yet he did not aspire to enter high society …'[164]

George gathered his friends to perform for Aird, in a superb example of his ability to tailor entertainment to meet individual taste. He had the private theatre, so he would fill it, rather than simply sit there with his piano. The cast consisted of his closest friends in the theatrical world: Arthur Cecil, Fred Leslie, Corney Grain, Durward Lely and Rutland Barrington. Aird must have been delighted that he had three Savoy stars in his home, along with other celebrities, and the play went very well, as George wrote: 'Although our actions were at times extravagant, still we played with great seriousness … A carroty wig and a red nose can no more make a comedian than a coat can make a man …'[165] He recalled that the twenty-minute piece went; 'with a roar of laughter from beginning to end.'[166]

The situation in 1889 then, as he left the Savoy, was that he was one of many piano entertainers. Many such artistes of that era are obscure today, but it is clear that there was a group at work in the last decades of the nineteenth century and in Edwardian years, all working the same seam. An obituary of 1951, on the death of Nelson Jackson, defines the category: 'Nelson Jackson who died last Thursday at the age of 80, was among the group of famous comedians who entertained at the piano in the early years of this century – the peer of such names as Harry Fragson, George Grossmith and Barclay Gammon. He was born in Liverpool, and first made his name there as a concert artist writing, composing and singing his own humorous songs ...'[167]

In August 1888 George made his entrance as an author. *A Society Clown* had been commissioned six months previously and George wasted no time in writing it; clearly he had a lot to say about his entertainer's life and in that work he stressed the social context and the professional considerations involved in such work. The publisher was James Williams Arrowsmith of Bristol, a Worcester man whose father had been a printer, and James took the firm from printing such things as shipping timetables to fiction and autobiography, and working as the official publishers for Bristol University. He was also a cricket enthusiast, and in the *Wisden Almanac* for 1913, his obituary noted that he was in the Harrow XI in 1868 and 1869, adding that an earlier appraisal of him had said, 'he is a brilliant field, returning the ball well at the wicket ... promises as he gets older to be a fine hitter.' He was President of the Gloucester County Ground Company also. But James fancied a plunge into literary publishing, and from 1871 he chanced his arm, eventually becoming the publisher of George and Weedon's *Diary of a Nobody*, and also of work by Jerome K Jerome and the famous adventure classic, *The Prisoner of Zenda*.

When he sat down to write his first memoir, George had a great deal of material on his life as a piano entertainer. As he told an interviewer for *The Pall Mall Gazette* in 1888, not long before he left the Savoy, he had what he called his 'Snob Book' and the interviewer explained that 'If you look through what Mr Grossmith calls his Snob Book you will find letters and cards from every prince, duke and peer in the kingdom.'[168] He took delight in filling *A Society Clown* with reminiscences of his entertaining in both high society and at various groups and concert halls across the country. As he confessed in the same interview, as the piece began with a line from 'a new Irish song' he was working on, many lyrics were written on the move: 'You have caught me composing a new Irish song with which I am going to astonish the natives. I always write the words in railway carriages. The motion seems to give me ideas.'[169]

The last decades of the nineteenth century opened up infinite opportunities for humour of all kinds, and perhaps most notably that individual kind which came from a crop of comedians, in the music halls and in all branches of theatre and entertainment. There was an affection for the surreal variety, often in pastiches and spoofs. This may be seen in such texts as the notebooks of Dan Leno, the variety star, who was as keen on 'Topsy Turvydom' as Gilbert or Grossmith. Like George, Dan carried around a notebook in which, as his first biographer noted, '... he recorded his freaks of fancy as they occurred to him ...'[170] His short scenes and rhymes contained both songs as bizarre as some of George's (such as one about a wasp and a hard-boiled egg) and also surreal, exaggerated social and historical dialogues which foreshadowed grotesque drama such as that of Alfred Jarry's *Pere Ubu*.

Yet George was a consummate businessman also: in *A Society Clown* he enumerates the range and category of performances in private homes, explaining that there were 'four to seven; afternoon parties and in contrast the late evening ones'. It is hard to resist the conclusion that he was more at home in these locations than on stage in London, as he wrote this reflection on his work as 'piano man':

'I never feel so much in my element as when I have a nice show on a dais, and a seated audience of sophisticated and well-dressed people, in a handsome drawing-room. It is a pleasure for me to sing to them; and although I occupy an hour and a half ... over the three musical sketches which I usually give, I feel a little sorry when I have finished.'[171]

He also explains that there were pressures and inconveniences, mainly at the kinds of classy affairs at which most of the crowd arrived very late and sat everywhere, even on the stairs, outside the room where he was singing.

Then there was the business of payment – something often embarrassing in the context of high society, when anything smacking of a 'service' with a kind of 'back door nature' necessarily involved lucre passing from palm to palm. George earned a great deal of money from his piano entertainments, but in that role he had to put up with delicate situations of this nature: 'Sometimes the hostess will thank me profusely and, in shaking hands, squeeze a little envelope into my palm. Some ladies will say loudly "Goodbye and thank you so much" then softly, "I will write to you tomorrow."'[172]

Describing his material and his special quality as an entertainer is not an easy task. A description of the Gaiety theatre star Leslie Henson, as written by James Agate in 1936, is probably close to what George must have been like: 'This is a buffoon of genius. Ask Leslie to poke fun at a seaside fortune-teller. Easy. Or make game of your Harley Street psychoanalyst. Easier still. Or take the mike out of the Sphinx. A sitter. Our buffoon has but one question for the lot: why must you be so utterly absurd?'[173] But of course this feature was only a part of it. One way to access his rare talent as a piano man and comic is through the writing, and we have ample evidence of that. Recordings by Leon Berger and Selwyn Tillett have helped a great deal in this, and one of these discs was done in association with the Gilbert and Sullivan Society, so there is a sound basis of research to them.

Two features of the songs are outstandingly important: the type of social commentary that works on ordinary human failings and foibles, along with the love he had for parody. There is plenty of visual documentation of his appearance in performance as well, so putting the two together enables the modern reader to make a reasonably accurate notion of a Grossmith entertainment. Pictures of him at the piano in the 1890s show him with hair parted down the middle as if cut with a knife, collar, cuffs and tie immaculate, pince-nez on a cord and handkerchief in the top pocket. His still at that time thin and wiry, and images of him actually playing stress his vivacity and movement, including one picture with the caption, 'Mr Grossmith drapes himself gracefully over the corner of the piano and proceeds to tell you all about it.'

His standing now is hard to ascertain. When assessed fifty years ago in Gervase Hughes' survey of *Composers of Operetta,* his limitations were clear. Hughes wrote: 'George Grossmith is now only remembered as having been what Anna Russell calls 'the little man who sings the patter song, but as an entertainer at the piano he was a lineal progenitor of the Norman Longs and B C Hilliams of our own day ... he actually collaborated with Gilbert in *Haste to the Wedding* ... Such an undertaking was really beyond his capabilities.'[174]

Basically, George was working in a world in which entertainment of a more highbrow verbal nature was rubbing shoulders with the more ribald presentations. In the 1890s, recitations began to be more appealing than ever, being successors to the Penny Readings. Anthologies and collections of 'recitations' were notably popular, and the material collected between the covers were often the work of well-known journalists of the mid to late years of the century, put alongside such classic writing as works by Sir Walter Scott and, naturally, Dickens. George's work at the piano, in sketches and in monologues, was closely linked to this, and amateurs and professionals were active in this cultural site of sharing words and stories. In 1893, for instance, F E Marshall Steele's anthology, *The Encore Reciter*, offered not only a large mix of writings, but an essay, very much in the manner of a style guide mixed with a coaching tone, perhaps as found in a drama club, headed 'Hints to Reciters.' Everything George did is in there, described and given with a layer of advice. The sections of the book are: 'Humorous Pieces,' 'Serious Pieces' and 'Dramatic Selections.' George's friend, F C Burnand, is included in the book, and Gilbert's verse is well represented. The advice extends to accents and dialects – the very things that George was adept at delivering – and even precise accounts of how to stand:

'As to position, stand erect, with one foot a few inches in front of the other, at an angle of something more than 45 degrees, each foot being turned slightly outwards. The arms should fall easily and gracefully by the side. Don't put your chin up in the air, please. Don't raise your eyes to gaze at the starry firmament … Don't close your fists. Don't spread your fingers, but curve them slightly …'[175]

All this highlights exactly how natural George was: he had to move a lot, and switch from being at the piano to move for a patter song.

The last decades of the century saw a boom in home entertainment of all kinds, but society parties were everywhere, often being extensions of the clubs and societies which existed for every profession, and George was a key member of an established fraternity of performers with a professional self-help network of their own. He explains in his memoir: 'I am frequently asked, when singing in private houses, if I am friendly with Mr Corney Grain … I had been suffering from a sore throat and could not fulfil a certain engagement, and he kindly sang in my stead. In return I sent him a small souvenir in the shape of a Tantalus.'[176]

There is also the question of George's agent, and the nature of theatrical and musical agents in general. For the two first major British tours after leaving the Savoy, George's agent was Narcisso Vert, based in London near Piccadilly. Vert's agency was to carry on under the leadership of his nephew, Pedro Tillett, who controlled the firm from 1905. D'Oyly Carte had an established musical agency, and would have worked with George had he had the time, and so when George first approached Vert at first, he told D'Oyly Carte what he was doing, to make sure he caused no offence.

Vert set up his business, along with three of his brothers, in Cork Street in 1886. Born in London in 1845, he was of Spanish descent, and obviously had a keen sense of business. He was later to manage such stars as Nellie Melba and even Sir Edward Elgar; he also worked at times with composers Grieg and Saint-Saens. Christopher Fifield, in his history of the Ibbs and Tillett 'musical empire' explains: 'Vert was very involved in the planning and construction of his artists' programmes. He could tell if a work or a song had been overexposed at a particular venue.'[177]

George was then set up to be away from home on tour for three quarters of the year. As Tony Joseph notes: 'Vert, who dealt with all the administrative side of the work, had procured him an engagement every day, afternoon and evening, five or six days a week right through – with the exception of a three week break at Christmas – to the following May.'[178]

The home entertainment extended to royalty, and on 12 November 1890, George entertained at Balmoral, and this memorable experience was to be, in a sense, just one more appointment in a demanding tour. It was far from being a long stay or a one-off particular engagement, although he did manage a short private conversation with her Majesty. In 1881 entertainments had resumed at Balmoral after a long period of mourning for Prince Albert who had died in 1861; F C Burnand's play *The Colonel* was performed in 1881 and Gilbert's *Sweethearts* in 1887. In 1890 it was George's turn. Not long before he arrived, there had been a performance of a comedy called *Used Up*, given in the ballroom before staff and local aristocrats, so George must have known that there was a sense of humour there and it would be no stiff, formal affair. But of course he was nervous, as he always was at a first performance.

The itinerary was demanding and the Queen's secretary, Sir Henry Ponsonby, wrote to explain the possibilities:

> 'As time is precious to you, I may explain that you can come by train which leaves Aberdeen at twelve twenty – or else somewhere about five – but this latter would not reach Balmoral till past eight p.m …We can give you a room here to sleep. But it is possible you may prefer to return to Ballater at night – eight miles so as to start by the earliest train …'[179]

Accounts of visits to Balmoral after the arrival of the railways still suggest a very difficult journey to be in the presence of Her Majesty. In 1850, the political secretary and diarist Charles Greville described his journey after being summoned to attend a council regarding the cholera epidemic: '… I started by the five o' clock train, dined at Birmingham, went on by the mail train to Crewe where I slept; breakfasted the next morning at Crewe hall, which I had never seen, and went on by the express to Perth, which I reached at half past twelve. I started on Wednesday morning at half past six and arrived at Balmoral exactly at half past two …'[180]

George did well and greatly pleased the Queen: she even asked for an encore – asking him to come back and sing his hit, 'See Me Dance the Polka'. George was given a special memento before he left: a watch chain with a monogram of VR in diamonds. Then he was on his way to the next Scottish venue at Aberdeen where university students were waiting to have a laugh and see a star from London. Regarding Her Majesty, one particular number from George, 'How the Ladies of the Future will Make Love' had the Queen 'in fits of laughter.'[181] Victoria loved what she called her 'treats' (theatricals) so much that there was an attempt by the royal photographer to capture them forever on film.[182]

George was also a favourite of Edward VII. As was noted previously, Edward loved giving dinners to actors and singers. Perhaps the most notable occasion was the dinner at Marlborough House in 1882, in which George appeared along with Irving, Arthur Cecil and others. The royal occasions give us proof that his work was adaptable to any audience, regardless of class or status.

Later, in the 1890s, George was also to have other managers but they were rather marginal figures in his life. In one eventful year, between 1897 and 1898, he had Frank Weathersby. Weathersby had a long pedigree in theatre history: his parents were well known at the old Haymarket theatre, and as a five-year-old, he had appeared in a melodrama. In his teens he played in panto and then by 1890 he was assistant stage manager for Lily Langtry when her company was at the St James's Theatre. He was part of Langtry's American tour in 1894, and played in *Charley's Aunt* in 1896, but then did some directing and for a year he managed both George and Weedon.

While managing the Grossmiths, Weathersby made a court appearance, and the case showed up the sometimes risky and exploitative nature of stage management. A man called Bosanquet obtained money by false pretences, advertising for 'amateurs, novices and beginners' to be employed in small parts on a theatrical tour. It was all bogus, and Weathersby was called as a witness to the court in Liverpool to testify, as it seemed that a certain 'Claud Broadbridge' whom he had meet years before, could have been one and the same man as 'Bosanquet.'[183]

Whoever the managers were, they had to sort out a hurried, non-stop tour of engagements, all varying in scale and revenue of course, but it was very profitable. Merely a few months on the road earned George more than he would have been paid at the Savoy. He was earning what would be, in the terms of 2013, around £200,000 per year.

Then came the United States. Mr Vert thought that it would be a grand idea for George to tour in the area between New York and parts of Canada. Rosa was to travel with him in spite of her tendency to suffer from sea-sickness. They talked it through and by October 1892 they were packed and ready to leave, on the *Teutonic*, leaving from Liverpool. The *Teutonic* was new, having been launched in January 1889, and having its maiden voyage to New York in August 1891. George and Rosa would have been in one of the 300 first-class cabins which were on the top three decks, and they were in one of the interconnected cabins for families, largely to cater for Rosa's need of quiet and rest when she was ill – and indeed she was after the stop at Queenstown (now Cobh) in Ireland where they would have taken on board around 800 emigrants. When they went out into the Atlantic, Rose was ill and kept a low profile, under the care of the doctor, while George, of course, socialised and took his place at the piano when needed.

The American tour opened in New York City at Chickering Hall, by Union Square on Fifth Avenue. The Hall had opened in

1875, with a capacity of 1,450, being a multi-purpose brownstone building which presented operas and serious lectures. Oscar Wilde appeared there, and it had also been the site of the first interstate phone call, made by Graham Bell himself, in 1877. George's usual nervous apprehensions began to prey upon him, as he gathered that the place was likely to burn down, and there was also some competition, because Marie Tempest, the singer and comedienne, was playing in the city as well. But all went well, after Vert had given George a boost and a pep-talk. In fact, Vert had retained some interest in George's career, and his various managers sometimes acted together, sharing responsibilities.

In New York he was fêted and lionised, and invited to become a member of various social clubs in which the acting fraternity gathered and networked. John Drew Jnr, the Shakespearean actor and President of the prestigious Players' Club, was apparently at the centre of the hearty welcome. Of course George would go down well in the United States: what one review called a performance by a 'dapper little fellow' was naturally an affectionate general response to that type of English humour that matched the dynamism, the sheer artistic openness, of the American enterprise at the time. When George moved on to Boston he experienced an audience of five thousand, and was staggered by the climate as well as by the reception and the sheer number of people who welcomed and loved his work.

Such a hugely impressive and grand experience could not fail to prompt from him some kind of response in terms of a piece of work, and sure enough, he wrote 'How I Discovered America'. He repeated the tour in 1894, and had absorbed so much from the experience that something had to be produced by way of a parody, such was his delight in sending up anything that was open to a risible interpretation or re-telling. The focus was on the inherent sentimentality in the tales and plays concerning traditional regional life (precursors of *The Waltons* etc). From this comes the song 'The Baby on the Shore' with its lines, *'In the far far west the sun was setting … we were thinking of the old folks at home/ and we left the baby on the shore.'*

In the midst of all the touring and the composing came an offer from Gilbert, who by this time was in need of a collaborator, as his partnership with Sullivan had ended after another disagreement. He had written a piece on which he was working with Alfred Cellier, but, being Gilbert – as tireless and productive as Grossmith – he also had another work awaiting a composer and writer of comic drama, a piece to be called *Haste to the Wedding*, and that was to be followed by *His Excellency*, in which George acted but was not involved in the writing.

Haste to the Wedding was an adaptation of an earlier Gilbert work. His other librettist was ill, but Gilbert clearly had George in mind in the new version – there was even some humour directed at his old pianist friend. The whole piece relies on a fusion of ridiculous farce while Tapping, a comic character being ridiculed, is in pursuit of a hat which is needed to save his wedding day, and the usual Gilbert absurdity. At one point in Act II Tapping is taken to be a certain Nisnardi, a piano entertainer, and George would have relished this passage from the scene:

> LADY P. And are you really Nisnardi?
> WOOD (aside) I must brazen it out (aloud) I am!
> LADY P. Incomparable falsettist!
> WOOD (aside) Good heavens, I'm a singer – a falsettist!
> Why I'm a bad baritone
> LADY P. And are you about to favour us with a
> specimen of your marvellous Talent?
> MARCH   Signor Nisnardi is most kindly going to sing
> three songs.[184]

It was surely a wonderful in-joke between George and Gilbert, and perhaps the audience also knew George's misgivings about his baritone voice, particularly if they had read *A Society Clown*, which was in print four years before *Haste to the Wedding*, which was presented at the Criterion Theatre on 27 July 1892. That production was significant for his son, GG, also: it was his stage debut, playing Young Foodle, and young GG would have seen his father down in the pit, conducting the orchestra. But unfortunately the play did not impress the critics. The run barely lasted a month, and the most damning comments came from *The Musical Times,* whose verdict was 'The public did not care for a good farce spoiled, or for music which had few redeeming features. Apparently it is not enough to be a writer and singer of comic songs in order to blossom forth as a composer of comic opera.'[185]

The Pall Mall Gazette, before the opening night, had 'a chat with Mr George Grossmith on his new opera' with the headline, 'The Society Clown as a Composer' and when the interviewer commented, 'You are not generally suspected of being a composer' George was playful in his reply: 'That's just another popular fallacy. Why nobody suspected me of being an acrobat and when I turned a cart-wheel it brought down the house.' He also pointed out that he had studied harmony with Edward Solomon. The interviewer persisted with his line of attack and pointed out that George had not much of a voice. The reply was the usual disarming one, with George saying that the songs written for him were on 'four or five notes, to encourage the others' when he worked at the Savoy.[186]

The reviews were generally indirect and restrained in their negative comments, but the audience were clearly not happy, as *The Era* noted: 'On Wednesday evening the response to *Haste to the Wedding* was generally enthusiastic, but there were a few who failed to see the drift of Mr Gilbert's drollery or to appreciate the tunefulness of Mr Grossmith's music and when these gentlemen appeared in response to the bulk of the audience's invitation, the dissentients made sarcastic remarks as to the verdict the critics would pass …'[187]

His Excellency brought George back on the stage for Gilbert, and this time the music was provided by Osmond Carr, a Yorkshireman who had written for burlesques, and who had also written for the impresario, George Edwardes at the Gaiety theatre In yet another 'topsy turvy' setting – Elsinore in Denmark – Gilbert cast George as Governor Griffenfeld, a man who lives to perpetrate practical jokes on a grand scale. George was attracted by the part of course, but also by the fact that old friends from the Savoy days were in the cast as well: Rutland Barrington, Jessie Bond and Alice Barnett. Gilbert had very strong set-piece patters for George as well, including the song 'Quixotic is his enterprise' in which comedy is analysed, around the theme of *And I've come to the conclusion that the mine of jocularity/In present anno domini, is worked completely out.'*

The practical jokes included fooling men into believing that they had been elevated to the peerage, and trying to place a strolling player as the 'Syndic' of the land – a chief justice or advocate. But in the end, the opera was marked down as another failure, and worse was the fact that George and Gilbert fell out about it. Letters were exchanged and feelings were expressed acrimoniously; it was really the end of George as a performer for Gilbert. In fact, although the audience welcomed him after such a long time away from the London stage, and the clearly very suitable role he had, the issue around which disagreements emerged was the accusation from Gilbert that George 'gagged- forgot his lines. It is completely understandable for today's reader, with the understanding of hindsight, that George was revelling in what he thought was a new freedom, but he had perhaps forgotten Gilbert's tight and insistent need to control everything, and George's response smacks of a man who has attained something as high and estimable as the status of Gilbert (the more famous). George wrote: 'I hold a position in my profession which is nearly equivalent to the one you hold in yours, and I expect to be treated with a certain amount of courtesy ...'[188]

A certain tone of overenthusiastic assertion was detectable in George's replies to the questions fired at him by the *Pall Mall Gazette* interviewer, referred to earlier, and it may not be going too far to suggest that the stresses and strains of the long-distance and intensive touring had taken an emotional toll on him. Through the whole episode of his working on the two Gilbert pieces there is a sense that George was ready to wind down, to taper his energies to the intimate entertaining he perhaps enjoyed the most. He gave his usual vigour and intelligence to the roles in those two pieces, but the results had been largely a failure, both as actor and composer. He surely felt, in his inner self, that the time had come to accept a less demanding lifestyle. He needed to see more of his family, which was seeing about as much of him as he had seen his father forty years earlier in the 'penny reading' days.

After all, in the year that he appeared in *Haste to the Wedding* he had made his debut, with Weedon, as a novelist. In fact, due recognition has not been given so far in my account of his career, to the celebrity status of George Grossmith, Savoyard star. By the early 1890s he was very widely known; as remarked earlier, he was very short (just above five feet tall) and always dapper and rather impressively dressed, though it would be inaccurate to call him a 'dandy.' With his hair plastered down flat, the pince-nez and the face of infinite range of expression, he was mobile, jocular and always a bundle of energy. During the years when he had left the Savoy and was on tour again, he had been writing – for *Punch*, and then *A Diary of a Nobody*, as well as his own sketches and short dramatic works. The next chapter will look at George, his brother Weedon and the ever-widening circle of friends around this man who was arguably, one of the most sociable, amusing and generous men of the theatre of his age. He had, one might say, not a single serious bone in his body. After describing the society man, attention will turn to his one undoubtable modern classic of comic fiction.

6

Circles of Friends

'What's the good of a home if you are never in it?
The Diary of a Nobody Chapter 1

In the Grossmith household in Dorset Square, as noted in my account of his life just after his marriage, the sheer scale and variety of his social connections was explained The Grossmith who was not only society clown but social conversationalist, celebrity and networker, was a formidable 'PR machine' to use modern terminology. There has been recently some attention paid to the notion of celebrity in the theatre and the cult of personality which has emerged over the last two centuries. The Grossmith home and club life, considered together, define his life and habits as being at the nexus of a number of cultural and artistic groups intermingling: in and around his home and clubs there were singers, writers, journalists, artists, actors, scientists and comedians. Such a context suggests a special, and yet also a typical, social round, with personality and performative, openly expressed bonds of friendship at the heart of things.

There is no doubt that George's huge social network was, at its core, a mutual admiration society, but also a self-help group too: friendship and clubbable habits meant that one could be called upon at any time to do a favour, to step in and save the day, keep up appearances. The brotherhood of actors, musicians and comics was solidly together in a commercial world in which battles were still in progress regarding copyright and plagiarism, but on the other hand, all the evidence points to an easy-going, tolerant attitude to 'earning a dollar' at a time when work was notoriously spasmodic. Even the burst of success brought about by a good run of a successful play or a popular tour, was seen as probably temporary in the long view of a whole career of struggle, and worse, or unpredictability.

One outstanding feature of George's life as a piano man was his interest in his earnings. He had seen his father go on the road, travelling across the provinces in order to keep earning, making the most of his particular talent, and the lesson had sunk in. In George's memoirs we have a sense of a man who had to perform and had to earn: the Dorset Square lifestyle and the large family had to be maintained. Although he was very well paid for his work, and became comfortably rich, it was all earned through a demanding schedule of work for most of the year, when he would be on trains, going from town to town.

George was both star and sociable friend. His life exhibits what Joseph Roach has called the establishment of 'public intimacy.' Roach explains:

> 'Celebrities, like kings, have two bodies – the body
> natural, which decays and dies, and the body politic,
> which does neither. But the immortal body of the 'image,'
> even though it is preserved on celluloid, on digitalised
> files or in the memory of the theatre-going public, always
> bears the nagging reminder of the former ... celebrities
> foreground a peculiar combination of strength and
> vulnerability ...'[189]

Roach digs deeper into theory, so that his thinking requires the creation of the terms 'charismata' and 'stigmata'- the former being a sign of strength and the latter being vulnerability. The notion of 'charismata' is useful, as is carries with it the suggestion that a combination of attractive features, working together, play a prominent part in defining and generating a performer's celebrity, or at least the actions, words and images related to him or her which convey celebrity.

At this time, celebrities in the world of comedy could earn vast amounts of money; Dan Leno, the music hall comic, is a perfect example. His first biographer gave instances of Leno's status:

> 'All this work brought him considerable fame and fortune.
> He revelled in both. He never tired of meeting his public
> in person, of being greeted in the street, of signing
> autographs and posing for photographers. Such was his
> fame and the potency of his name that both a saloon bar
> and a comic newspaper were named after him, and he was
> delighted to open the former in person – at the Scarboro
> Hotel in Leeds – and appear to be the actual editor of the
> latter.'[190]

In George's case, there is no doubt that he cultivated a social persona every time he left for stage, club, dinner or party, whether the people awaiting him were royalty or a seaside holiday audience. He was as 'dramatic' and self-conscious as an artist as Oscar Wilde, who at this time showed the world how notoriety and celebrity rubbed shoulders in every context, illustrating Wilde's own saying that not being talked about was worse than being talked about. In other words, though George cannot be accused of self-seeking vanity or relentless promotion of the image he knew he had, undoubtedly he was aware that once there was a persona in public, that had to be maintained at all costs. People knew what they wanted to see and hear and the celebrity had to keep on delivering that commodity. This is not to say that he was uncomfortable in this role: on the contrary, all the available pictures of him, and consequent interviews, depict a man at home with the traditional drawing-room smartness expected of a society entertainer. But my reasoning is that his immaculate cuffs, ties and collars were as much a part of his entertainer's persona as anything seen on Dan Leno or Marie Lloyd in the music halls.

If we add to this picture the George Grossmith who was acutely attuned to topicality, vogues and fads, then we have an artist who found in society and in his sub-cultures in the spectrum of the broad range of arts in his time, a supreme example of the gentle satirist: his songs rely greatly on a multiplicity of accents across the social strata of his time, from the mock-Irish of 'His Nose was on the Mantelpiece' to the seaside context of 'I Don't Mind Flies.' He had no problem with making fun of the French and the Germans, and fun taken from supposed national stereotypes was fairly general. The Queen herself, who was of German descent and who, of course, married a German, loved making fun of German cultural pursuits.

He also had his finger on the pulse in terms of social commentary, such as his song on 'How I Became a Detective' from his sketch, *Castle Bang or Where's the Heiress?* in which his social stereotypes extend to the then fashionably fascinating new version of the detective in a world of political intrigue, Fenian activity and espionage. But above all, what rests easily in his songs is the same quality found in his satires and in Charles Pooter, the 'Nobody' of his classic novel – the celebration of a certain quintessential Englishness, the version bound by the four walls of home and the little dramas and pleasures of the routine, circumscribed life.

Freemasonry in George's life was very important, and in that aspect of his socialising, he was fairly typical of the middle-class man of his time. The Masonic lodge had a place as important for the Grossmith circle as their clubs. As Andrew Prescott has explained:

' … the establishment of a Masonic lodge provided
a means by which the new professional classes could
socialise in a neutral atmosphere after work. Thus,
members of the London School Board petitioned for the
establishment of a Masonic Lodge so that they could relax
after committee meetings were finished. Similar Lodges
were established for other professional groups …'[191]

The 1890s, as a study of any cluster of periodicals of the time will illustrate, provided aspiring middle-class people, from those in lower echelons of commerce to those in the established professions, with a bewildering array of sites in which social connections could be established. George, typical of his time, would most likely be found at the Beefsteak Club or at a Lodge if he were not at home or on tour. The evidence shows that he was a homely type when he could make the time, and he revelled in children, everyday husbandry around the house, pets and bicycles, as much as any man, in spite of this hunger for society and for the cultivation of his social persona.

Yet there is no doubt that he gloried in his value and respect, his sheer high status among so many friends. At the end of *A Society Clown* he lists and prints several letters to him from people across the spectrum of society as he knew it. One of these relates to a specific group, brought close to him partly by his work for *Punch* and partly by connections in Weedon's life: the world of the Victorian artist. The letter in question is from Frank Holl:

'My Dear Grossmith,
If you are not too tired and have no better engagement,
will you come and see my "show" – all portraits (chamber
of horrors) before they go to the R.A. on Friday evening?
The usual business – not dress.'

This little note illustrates the tone and special feel we have of the artistic fraternity, in its widest sense, of George's 1890s community. Weedon, who was always going to be an artist, followed the then common trajectory of starting by painting narrative or genre pictures, and then switched to portraits through the need to earn money. At times, he did very well in this, and his friend Holl followed exactly the same course, though succeeding markedly in his profession. While Weedon was struggling to set up on his own, Holl offered him financial help, and the network was established; Holl become a friend to George also. In the last decades of the century, activities involving drawing and writing were often fused, and many writers (Gilbert, for instance) were skilled at line drawing. Humorists in literary forms in particular often either mixed writing and drawing or at least worked with artists.

Weedon started out (after basic schooling) at the West London School of Art in Bolsover Street. In the mid- and late-Victorian years, the area was popular with artists, who set up studios there, most notably Sir David Wilkie. From friends such as Holl, Weedon would have soon learned how much financial survival depended on patronage, and the rising ranks of the new middle class were eager for portraits for their wall. Even the wealthier working classes (such as Charles Pooter, in *The Diary of a Nobody*) felt the need to have a portrait or at least a photo from a studio of themselves on the wall. Holl had at first taken his art very seriously, going to great lengths to achieve the realism he wanted in his narrative and genre paintings, and in his early stage as a painter, Weedon would have done something of the same, but not to the same extent, as Paula Gillett explains, with reference to Holl's painting, Newgate: Committed for Trial: 'It was painted inside the prison after the artist had himself locked in a cell so that he could experience the feeling of imprisonment.' [192]

Weedon wrote at length in his autobiography, *From Studio to Stage*, about his struggle to succeed in the art world: he gravitated to acting as a means of earning a living after portrait painting and the maintenance of his studio proved too demanding. We shall return to Weedon's acting in the next chapter.

What about George's other circles, adjoining the world of art and illustration? In the social milieu of the acting fraternity, the camaraderie was intense and varied, and included both sexes. The newspapers from the 1870s to the early Edwardian years, were always listing events in which George and friends took part: these ranged from charity and benefit concerts to dinners. Regulars at these assemblies were George's fellow actors from the Savoy years, along with Toole and his other regular thespians from all corners of the theatrical world. Like his father before him, George could be relied on to lead a discussion, give a comic speech, and as with his life in the clubs, he would give a toast, as in the dinner given for the New Vagabonds Club in the King's Hall of the Holborn restaurant in December 1897, when Lord Charles Beresford was the special guest and 'Mr George Grossmith proposed the toast of "the ladies" to which Mr James Buddlesworth replied.'[193]

A year later, in the Christmas celebrations, we find him as part of an entertainment at St George's Hall in Langham Place, working with Brandon Thomas and Lotte Venne, rubbing shoulders with a variety act called 'The Japs' who were masked minstrels, derived from the 'nigger minstrel bands' of the halls. The review in *The Times* gives us a good idea of how George mixed with any other entertainer; we also learn a typical sampling of his programmes:

'The remaining part of the programme is occupied by Mr George Grossmith, who gives one of his amusing musical sketches on the subject of "Awful Bores" one has no difficulty in recognising the bores Mr Grossmith describes except when he ranks himself among them and one can only wish that they amused one as much when encountered outside the St George's Hall. Mr Grossmith's presentment of the vicar who is trying to compose his sermon amid constant interruptions, and the young man who is having his photograph taken, are excellent pieces of character acting ...'[194]

George sang at least three songs as well as doing these sketches, including 'The Vacillating Waltz', 'The Wife who sat UP' and 'The Tune that Haunted Me'.

In 1899, at the meeting of the New Vagabonds at their Club, the Grossmith circle widened to include Mark Twain, on one of his periodic trips to London where he lectured. There was more than a passing resemblance between Grossmith and Twain, the main similarity being in their incessant and compulsive need to send up everything and engage in skits and parodies. George clearly warmed to Twain. On this occasion, it was a 'ladies' night' and George was in the chair. Sitting beside him were Conan Doyle, Douglas Sladen and G H Burgin. In George's speech, he asserted that American storytellers were more concise and direct that their English counterparts; he told the audience that years before, when he first sat to listen to Mr Twain, he made notes.

Twain stood and replied to George, pointing out that taking those notes was 'just like Mr Grossmith ... he took what he could get!' Then he proceeded to make fun of various notions of morality.[195]

George and friends were part of a network of stars who all sent up each other and revelled in fun wherever they could create it. When George was interviewed about his book *Piano and I* and about his tour in 1890, the interviewer wrote: 'The subjects of Mr Grossmith's imitations include Mr Corney Grain, Signor Tosti, Mr Lawrence Kelly, Mr Arthur Roberts, Isidore de Lara etc. From none of these has any protest against the imitations come ...' In the same interview, George made a point of explaining that before imitating Irving, he had written to his friend to ask permission. Irving replied: 'Go ahead my dear Grossmith, and peace be with you!'[196]

George had so many friends among the ranks of journalists that it is hard to select any for special mention, with the exception of Frank Burnand and Andrew Halliday. Burnand, as the editor of *Punch* between 1880 and 1906, had encouraged George and had published his *Very Trying* sketches, based on the Bow Street reporting, and the first short extracts from what would later become *The Diary of a Nobody*. Burnand, born in London, also wrote for the stage, producing mainly farces, but he was the author of *Cox and Box,* and hence that was his first connection with George. That was in 1866, and Sullivan had written the music. In an adaptation of that piece, George played at the Lyceum in a charity event; and he had a patter song – something that helped to bring him to the attention of Gilbert and Sullivan. In such a way does 'networking' perhaps mixed with chance and forge careers. In George's case, one may argue that simply by being constantly busy, and always socialising and making people laugh, he made his own luck. In the sense that he forged out his opportunities to be noticed, there is some truth in that view.

George knew Andrew Halliday through his father, particularly in connection with the Savage Club, as Halliday was one of the founders of that society, in 1857. He produced burlesques, and wrote for Dickens' *All The Year Round*. George wrote that he met and made friends with Halliday 'under the parental roof.'[197] In effect, through his father's social circles, George laid the foundations of his own later on, and Halliday represented, along with other such as Artemis Ward, creative types from the generation before that of George, Grain and Barrington, but all rubbed shoulders in clubs and at dinners.

George had published the *Very Trying* pastiches of court dramas, in *Punch* in 1884. In the last twenty years of the century, courtroom experience had become a very popular subject for journalists and writers. Collections of 'courtroom romances' appeared, along with true crime genre collections of famous court cases. Frank Burnand and George had realised this, and the fascinating magistrate Flowers, who had presided over much of the material George reported on, is written in the sketches as 'Bowers.' A typical extract is this little interchange between Bowers and a defendant:

> Bowers: Now is your time to ask any question of the witness.
> Defendant: Thanks, your Worship. (to witness) What's your name?
> Complainant: Short
> Defendant: All right, I'll soon make short work of you.
> (*Roars of laughter in which the magistrate joins*)
> Complainant (*indignantly*) I don't consider this a case for joking your Worship
> Mr Bowers: You are right there: but I can't, in justice, rebuke a man for joking when I've been doing it myself ...'[198]

The nineteenth century closed for George, though, with a family event: on 8 June 1900, George's daughter Sylvia married James Bevan, a barrister at the Middle Temple, at Marylebone Parish Church. She was just twenty-five, having been born on 23 September 1875. *The Era* reported: 'It was a pretty wedding as a marriage in "the" profession invariably is. Three clergymen tied the marriage knot and the toilets of the ladies might have excited the envy of the enclosure at Ascot. The circle of friends included a cluster of celebrities of the stage and literature, including Adelina Patti, Mrs Braddon, the Bancrofts, Toole and Harry Lawson.'[199] There was an even more impressive group at the reception, given at home in Dorset Square, as the same paper later added, pointing out that at that venue there were aristocracy as well as thespians, and these included Lord Edward Spencer Churchill, Sir James and Lady Crichton Browne and Baroness Burdett Coutts.

George also found time to work with Arthur Law, a prolific writer of farces, who had been part of the German-Reed entertainments, often teaming up with Corney Grain. Law would write the drama as the main attraction, and Grain would add a sketch, as in 1879 when they toured with the Reeds and on offer was Law's *One Hundred Pounds Reward*, along with Grain's *Our Calico Ball*. In 1880, Arthur married Fanny Holland, who had featured in many of his sketches, notably as a deaf old lady in *Wanted: A Lady's Companion* in 1880 Law became well known for his play *The New Boy*, which enjoyed a huge success. He was in many ways a kindred spirit to George, and they did well together, principally in producing *Uncle Samuel* as an opener at the Savoy, and later *Mr Guffin's Elopement*, which was written for J L Toole, in 1882. Law had at one time served in the army, and like Grain, found a second career in the theatre.

By that year, George Grossmith was not only the 'Society Clown' and former Savoy Star: he was the celebrated co-author of *The Diary of a Nobody*, and we must turn to that work next, retracing our steps back to 1892. As the century turned, the Grossmiths were well and truly established on the stage, with both Weedon and GG established as actors. Weedon was to write another novel, now very much forgotten, but George and Weedon's piece of light satire was to become a major classic of humorous literature.

7

GEORGE, WEEDON AND
THE DIARY OF A NOBODY

'To be happy is to be perpetually employed'
Thomas Gray

O n 29 May 1894, Weedon wrote from his office at the Vaudeville Theatre to a Mrs Tweedie: 'I am so sorry that I am engaged on 10th otherwise I should have been so delighted' and he added, 'Glad you liked the party.'[200] Like his brother, and like Corney Grain in fact, he was now a very busy actor-manager, having turned to this from his earlier attempts to succeed as an artist. He had hit the theatrical headlines four years previously, acting in Arthur Pinero's play, *The Cabinet Minister,* at the Court Theatre, in which he played Mr Lebanon, 'the little money-lending cad' as *The Daily Graphic* described him. His acting ability was described by the great theatre critic, James Agate, in an essay in his collection, *Buzz Buzz!*:

> 'It is not claimed for Mr Grossmith that he has the
> explicit gift of pathos, but rather that his comedy... is
> become the pathetic, or as good. The face is wonderful.
> The actor has not sponged all expression from it, as
> Coquelin did, remodelling the clay at every new character.
> Mr Grossmith has not got "the bunch of countenances,"
> but he has evolved, superbly, a mask, a permanent actor's
> mask, to fit the trivialities, smallnesses, self-sufficiencies of
> his Tidmarshes and Preedys.'[201]

To be noticed by Agate was an achievement in itself; Weedon had become the small bundle of energy that his brother had established as a major part of his stage persona. They were both very short, but blessed with expressive faces, a talent for mimicry, and an infallible comic sense of the ridiculous. Life in the theatre certainly did not always go well. In June 1895, when he was managing the Vaudeville, he was faced with a flop, as *The Stage* reported: 'Mr W Grossmith says frankly that his present play does not satisfy the box office and his new piece not being ready he had decided to close his season on Saturday June 15 and has sub-let the theatre to Mr Frederick Kerr.'[202]

Weedon surely relished the project of providing the drawings for *The Diary of a Nobody*. He had worked as a portraitist for many years before working with his brother on the book, and clearly, as he had shown in his line drawings for *Punch* magazine, he was the ideal partner for George in creating the comic image of Pooter. The book was published in 1892, after parts of it had appeared in *Punch*, filling two half-columns, in early 1888. He had clearly felt the frustration of not having become the painter he always wanted to be. After all, he had been a student at the Royal Academy Schools and his portrait of his father, reading *The Pickwick Papers* had been hung at the Academy. Then, a little later after setting himself up in his studio, he worked long and hard on a massive painting called Till Daylight Doth Appear, which was a work with a historical theme (what the serious artist was supposed to aspire to do, but that had been rejected by the Academy.

After that came the friendship with Holl and the portraits, but after his first part working for D'Oyly Carte, he joined the company led by Rosina Vokes in Liverpool, and in 1887 appeared for Irving as Jacques Strop in *Robert Macaire*, and from that point, plenty of work came his way. But his finger was surely itching to work on drawing and painting. Depicting the people in George's fictional Pooter family of The Laurels, Brickfield Terrace, Holloway, was just the ticket, and the brothers produced something special.

Up to the time of the special edition of 1924, still printed by Arrowsmith, its original publisher, the *Diary* had gone through six editions, and between October 1910 and September 1919 it was reprinted ten times. Some writers of the 1890s were determined to employ realistic approaches to a clearly conceived aim, as was the case with George Gissing, who wrote that he wanted to deal with 'the essentially unheroic, with the day-to-day life of the vast majority of people who are at the mercy of paltry circumstance …'[203] George may have thought in the same way, but that cannot be known. There is no secondary commentary; there are no author interviews with in-depth explanations. On top of that, the book's diary-form eclipses the author, fulfilling Flaubert's dictum that the author of a novel should be everywhere but never visible. In other words, the *Diary* comes from the same instinctive urge to create humour with George's eye firmly focused on the kinds of subjects which satire has always attended to: folly, arrogance, falsity and mendacity. The novel has these and other human frailties as well, but it is more: there is a universal quality in Charles Pooter, the loyal City clerk, that stretches his stature to something between Everyman and the 'little man' of so much literature, across the globe – not merely in English writing.

J.W.Arrowsmith, the Bristol-based publisher of the *Diary*, was doing very well, after expanding from practical guides and university publishing. His venture into fiction had been a smart move. In 1895 he was interviewed for *The Sketch* when he had just secured Rider Haggard for one of his publications, an annual anthology. He explained that 'My most successful ventures have been in the sphere of fiction … Readers of fiction at the time [c1890] wanted something less cumbersome than the three-volume novel – something that would be at once crisp, fresh and absorbing.'[204] His first real success, *Three Men in a Boat*, he said 'soon ran up to 140,000' and he also published W G Grace on cricket, and that sold over 11,000 very quickly. He told the interviewer than 'Nine large machines are constantly running on book work.'[205] Nine years before he published the *Diary*, he had had huge success with a local author, Hugh Conway, selling over 400,000 copies of his novel *Called Back*.[206]

The basis of having a narrative voice of absolute ordinary plainness, the self-regarding tone that assumes no other reader but the self, is the foundation for everything else in the book. It mirrors the established genre of such diaries, as in, for instance, these entries from the massive diary of the nineteenth century's Pepys, Charles Greville:

> April 1st I came to London on Sunday night with
> Berkeley Craven. The world is very dull and everything
> much as it always is.
> August 4th I went to Oatlands. There was a very large
> party … we played whist till four in the morning…
> Oatlands is the worst managed establishment in England;
> there are a great many servants, and nobody waits on you,
> a vast number of horses and none to ride or drive.[207]

The title of the book was not George's invention: as George noted, 'The excellent title was suggested by our mutual friend, F C Burnand' (the dedication in the first edition). That title fits the style and content perfectly. What George created was the immediate materiality of existence, something intimately bound up with the life of an employee who has to dress appropriately and present an image to the world. That materiality is, in George's hands, something in an environment that must be controlled and mastered, and it is close to the actual autobiographical writing of real clerks of the time, such as C H Rolph, who wrote: 'At about this time it was decided that I should have my very own made-to-measure suit. It was to be made by an old friend of the family, Mr C Dell of Dawes Road, Fulham, who pout himself forward as a Bespoke Tailor.' That is essentially a Pooterish sentence.[208]

The novel on one level may be seen as an examination of captivity, framed in a context of ultimate enterprise and commercial revolution. The voice we read and follow is that of a prisoner of safety, of total devotion to another; Pooter's personality is as much imprisoned as the convict in Pentonville. Yet, as the contrast with his son Lupin shows, the cell is self-made. The frame of the story is one of reduction, the imposed reductive life of the man 'with no qualities' as this was phrased later by another novelist, Robert Musil. Yet there is a saving factor, something that redeems Pooter and all he stands for: he is, like Aristotle's tragic hero, *like us but not of us*. The narrative device of the diary gives George the flexibility to let the voice of Pooter enter anywhere in consciousness, and that site of selfhood is known to us all.

It would be a mistake to take Pooter as simply a version of Marx's enslaved proletarian, selling his labour in order to be 'born free but in chains' to paraphrase Voltaire. On the contrary, Pooter finds satisfaction, and even beauty, in his imposed control of his small, circumscribed life. Reading the book at another level, that of taking it as a work embedded in its time, hooking into the immediate social context, is more rewarding. George puts all the important aspects of the clerk's lifestyle into the *Diary*: the Volunteer ball, the reliance on tradesmen, the Sunday walks and their restrictions, Lupin's theatricals and gambling and so on, and these are all linked to the focus of the narrative, which is how Pooter survives without allowing his moral structures to be eroded.

The challenges, perils and risks related to the life of the city clerk give the book its relentless nature as a tale of the little man caught up in a world he thinks is framed and defined on trust and right behaviour. His life as a city clerk is very much an occupation that had gradually developed in scale throughout the century. Dickens had taken a great interest in these office slaves who kept the wheels of commerce turning, and in the character of Wemmick in *Great Expectations*, he had understood the growing importance of the dichotomy of work/home for that class. Wemmick retires to his home as to a stronghold, that place of retreat being like a castle within London's great mass. As the suburbs expanded, along with the new railways, in the last two decades of the century, so the city clerks became rooted on the periphery, with a commuter's journey to make every day except Sunday.

In that context, the health and recreation of the clerk became important. Five years before the *Diary* was published, the Kyrle Society, founded in 1876 by Miranda and Octavia Hill, with the aim of improving and enriching working people's lives through healthy open-air pursuits and a fulfilled domestic life, issued a statement about the lanes and field-paths near London. Their report had this plea to local authorities: 'Speaking generally, communications outward from the metropolis towards any open space, or between any open space and the neighbouring railway stations ... are those which it would seem most essential to preserve; in some cases a circular walk would be of great value.'[209] It will be recalled that Pooter, walking with his friends, is not allowed through a gate leading to a pub because he is from Holloway. But there were other fears for the health and happiness of the clerks, relating to their long hours of concentrated work, and nothing was really to happen of any significance until the years just before the Great War. In 1913 the Medical Officer of Health for the City wrote in response to the perceived failure of the 1912 Railway offices Bill to address health problems of clerks: 'The Medical Officer of Health says that the requirements of the Bill are a step in the right direction, but it is difficult to understand why they should be restricted to railway offices only. Could they be extended to all offices where clerks and other persons are employed, their utility would soon become apparent ...'[210]

Of course, Pooter has to be defined as lower middle class: he employs a housemaid, Sarah. In the 1890s there was a huge demand for maids, cooks and educational services for the expanding clerk commuter class out in the suburbs, and the new clerks and their families were, of course, aspirational. That places Pooter in a classification which is deeply interesting within fiction: he is in flux, a person working to be transmuted into something permanent or at least higher in the scale of things. When eventually, Mr Perkupp, his boss, obtains Pooter's house as a gift for his long-serving employee, the jubilation is triumphant, calling for two bottles of champagne from the local merchant. Again, the growth of the suburbs in the 1890s has information that backs up the importance of this gift: developers were busy at that time buying properties to improve and let. A typical advertisement was one offering a line of properties, semi-detached, such as a group of six in Holloway advertised in 1890 which would bring in a total of £252 per annum. Pooter would probably have paid around £40 annual rent for The Laurels. His housemaid would have earned around £16 per annum (perhaps £800 today).

Pooter lives for control in the smallest things; he is arguably the 'new man' of the time in that he cares about gardening and interior decoration; his hobbies and household recreations, social circle and self-development define his aspirational nature. His class was tasting 'culture' as something perceived as being a cut above the art and entertainment of manual workers. Pooter expects his free tickets to the theatre to be for a solid, social-realist piece of drama at a respectable theatre, but instead he is thrown among the everyday punters at a place just a shade above a music hall.

Where does the real fictional interest lie then? George aims to bring the reader gently in, positioned to share in the satirical enterprise of laughing at the follies and absurdities of Pooter's striving to hold The Laurels and his lifestyle at all costs: after all, there are threats from every quarter, most of these being caused by his son Lupin, after his return home from being sacked from his clerking at a firm up north in Oldham. The threats to stability and success are largely focused on Pooter's job and the power of Mr Perkupp.

This interest is also something which is part of a larger picture, a factor in the literature of the time. George as usual, was finely attuned to topical preoccupations and trends. Lynne Hapgood, in her study of suburban fiction of the periods, identifies the dominant themes in this literary context, in her discussion of Arnold Bennett's first novel:

'All the themes of suburban fiction are interwoven in
A Man from the North:the nature of masculinity, the
need for love and its corollaries, marriage, children and
domesticity; the ambition and optimism of youth; upward
mobility and class redefinition. [211]

Hapgood sees and explains the recurrent difficulty in judging and placing the book in that sub-genre of suburban fiction: 'Because

Pooter has become synonymous with modern definitions of suburban identity – boring, respectable, full of inflated self-importance and a social climber obsessed with outward show – it is almost impossible to criticise the class orientation of the *Diary* … without seeming to be unable to get the joke …'[212]

There is also, as in all successful storytelling, the axis of oppositional forces throughout the novel, and the strongest of all is the generational one of father and son with entirely opposing attitudes. When Lupin is employed by Gylterson and Sons, after being sacked from Perkupp's firm, this happens:

'To my amazement I read that Gylterson and Sons had absolutely engaged Lupin at a salary of £200 a year, with other advantages. I read the letter through three times and thought it must have been for me … I was silent. Lupin said, 'What price Perkupp now? You take my tip, Guv -"off" with Perkupp and freeze onto Gylterson, the firm of the future! … The stagnant dummies have been standing still for   years.'[213]

The attraction of the new attitudes – the temptation to gamble and speculate, which Lupin had earlier tried and lost money for others – was a constant problem for the City clerks in the late Victorian and Edwardian years, and George was fully aware of this. Lupin has dabbled in that speculation and had his fingers burned, as so many did. In the year in which the *Diary* was being written, there were several court cases brought about by stock market speculation among clerks, such as this in June 1891 when Beriro v Thalheim came before the Lord Mayor's Court. Two City clerks had shared a venture, investing in King Solomon's Mines Ltd and in East London railway shares. It all went sadly wrong, and the court reporter summed up the outcome:

'The shares were carried over and they continued to fall until the total loss was £203.12s 3 d [£20,000 in 2013] In this loss the plaintiff said that the defendant had agreed to pay half. He had paid some of it by instalments and he had taken the money when there was any balance in his favour.'[214]

The judge decided that it was a pure gambling contract like a horse race, and he found for the defendant. Such cases were frequent: this was an era of frenzied investment, as Lupin's life shows. But he succeeds by the end of the novel through a secondary means to riches and security – networking with the wealthy.

From Lupin's success in that sphere comes the ultimate irony of the book: Pooter has tried hard to be a participant in 'society' in the sense of what Regency people would have understood as '*high ton*.' Implicit in Pooter's delight at being invited to the Lord Mayor's Ball or to the Volunteers' ball is his belief that mixing in the right company will bring about promotion, fruitful contacts and some enhancement of one's status. Yet he does not even understand the nature of the Masonic structures within the 'society' he so much desires, as when, at the Lord Mayor's ball, we have this scene, featuring the rude Farmerson, the ironmonger:

> 'Before I could think of a reply, one of the sheriffs, in full Court costume, slapped Farmerson on the back and hailed him as an old friend, and asked him to dine with him at his lodge. I was astonished. For full five minutes they stood roaring with laughter, and stood digging each other in the ribs. They kept telling each other they didn't look a day older. They began embracing each other and drinking champagne.'[215]

If anyone at the time understood the importance of the 'brotherhood' in a profession, it was George Grossmith. But again, as Lynne Hapgood's observations show, the reader positioning is very subtle, emanating from the clever duality in the nature of the narrative.

The focus of attention for Pooter inside this context of social change, generational conflict and aspirations, is home. The notion was a very central and often contentious one at the turn of the nineteenth century. In some respects, there was a turn away from the suburban identity by writers who wanted 'home' and its associations to be quite the opposite of any city life, and they saw suburban life as an unacceptable compromise in that respect. Nine years before Pooter's diary there was Richard Jefferies' autobiography *The Story of My Heart* which has one of the clearest statement about this dissatisfaction with 'home' as a city dweller might perceive it. Jefferies recounts how he was 'much in London' and he was wandering in what green spaces he could find, and then this leads to the kind of vision that Pooter would never have understood: 'The bright morning sun of summer heated the eastern parapet of London Bridge ... The broad water was a smooth sheen of light, the built-up river flowed calm and silent by a thousand doors ... I felt the felt the presence of the immense powers of the universe ...'[216]

Somerset Maugham, a young trainee doctor in London keeping his writer's diary in 1900, was capable of writing: 'London. The western clouds of the sunset were like the vast wing of an archangel, flying through the void on an errand of vengeance: and the fiery shadow cast a lurid light upon the city.'[217] Poor Pooter does not have that poetic faculty, certainly not 'writ large' – but he does take pleasure in the beauty of small things.

Pooter's sense of his world may lack vision, but he is sure that home equals happiness, and the 'new man' should adorn it. In a strange, surreal way, his attempts to paint his bath red (leading to disaster of course) are expressions of his creativity – something that generally goes awry, as it does for most. Yet c1890-1910, in that quiet before the storm, when people were experiencing the mass consciousness of suburban identity, home was the one icon of stability, something evocative of a pre-industrial age, even if its offerings were little more than a square of earth for a few flowers: 'I procured and sowed some half-hardy annuals in what I fancy will be a warm, sunny border.'[218]

All Pooter's attention is given to the preservation and adornment of his own space – a home in a sense that had not been seen as such before for any variety of labouring proletarian or middle-class pen-pusher. In the literature of the period, time and again writers contrast the rush, ebb and flow of human traffic in the metropolis and the estranging character of the workplace, with constructs of 'home.' One of the most sustained examples of this is in Richard Church's lengthy autobiographical enterprise which formed his trilogy of books on the genesis of a writer. He uses as his epigraph to the third volume, *The Voyage Home*, in which he looks back to his office work c1900, a quote from Clara Schumann written to Brahms: 'The concept of earthly happiness is, after all, bound up with life in the home.'[219] Church's book is mostly a mixture of elegy and celebration of home as it was when he first started, as an office worker. At the heart of his memoir is this assertion of the importance of home: 'The habit, the craving or instinct, cuts close and intimately into our lives. On outside directive, of politics, religion or economic necessity can wholly destroy it. A child in an orphanage will create a pathetic hiding-place, a mouse's nest, where he may be alone with his possessions, and thus assured of that universe.'[220]

Compare this articulate and rhetorical style, and we see the paucity in Pooter: we understand that he has the certainty that his home is central to everything he desires and preserves, but – and this is fundamental to George's conception of his book – Pooter has no voice to express anything beyond the banal. It is in that reductive language that the real power of the *Diary* lies. Hence the appropriate potency and irony of the word 'nobody.' There is a nagging insistence that in a sense, when all social imagery and decoration are taken away, he is Everyman. This is what perhaps prompted J C Squire to say, in his introduction to the 1924 edition: '... the fact remains as it seems to me, that a large area of English social life is painted in this book more faithfully and fully than anywhere else.'[221]

'Home' in every sense was prominent in the mediation of cultural life of the 1880s and 1890s, and books such as Clarence Cook's *House Beautiful* (1878, reprinted twice in 1883) expresses notions of the importance and adornment of home in a style reminiscent of Pooter's voice. The book begins with a poem by Robert Herrick as an epigraph, Thanksgiving for this House:

'Lord, Thou hast given me a cell
Wherein to dwell;
A little house, whose humble roof
Is weatherproof,
Under the stars of which I lie
Both soft and dry ...'

The lines are open to the same bathos we may draw from Pooter's simple and pithy sentences which encapsulate the limits of his philosophical reflection. Cook writes with the same sense of mock adventure, as if the creative adornment of the home is a major enterprise: 'Whoever will try the experiment will find the reward in peace and serenity and real comfort.' He is speaking of carpets here, as opposed to rugs.[222]

Before we even read the first page, the ultimate irony of the manner in which George achieved all this home-making and this striving for respectability strikes us in Pooter's supposed little note to his readers: 'Why should I not publish my diary? I have often seen reminiscences of people I have never heard of, and I fail to see – because I do not happen to be a 'somebody' – why my diary should not be interesting. My only regret is that I did not commence it when I was a youth.'[223] In this way, the pretence of verisimilitude – the same ploy as Charlotte Bronte's calling *Jane Eyre* an 'autobiography ' on the title page – sets the reader's mind somewhere between a shared reality and an invitation to laugh at such a voice from the obscurity from which it declares it belongs.

Naturally, attention must turn to Carrie, Mrs Pooter. She gladly joins in with everything Pooter plans and does; in a sense they are two innocents let loose in a world which has a moral slippage inherent in it, and so Carrie is partly a steady centre of rightness for which Pooter has to reach for support and confirmation of his actions. But more importantly Carrie is a mother-figure, the one who acts like the inner voice commenting on his folly and shortcomings, as in the aftermath of his painting obsession: 'Woke up with a fearful headache and strong symptoms of a cold. Carrie, with a perversity which is just like her, said it was "painter's colic" and was the result of my having spent the last few days with my nose over a paint-pot.'[224]

However, she is also undoubtedly the object of his genuine and constant affection, though in terms in which the modern reader would see as narrow and paternalistic. In a succession of petty tribulations, he writes of her as the 'eternal feminine' in his little universe of male affairs, the world of business, kept at a distance from her. This is seen at the Mansion House ball: 'As it takes two to make a quarrel, and as it was neither the time nor the place for it, I gave my arm to Carrie and said, "I hope my darling little wife will dance with me, if only for the sake of saying we had danced at the Mansion House as guests of the Lord Mayor."'[225]

There is also the question about whether or not Weedon was contributor or part-author of the book, in addition to supplying the illustrations. There is no doubt that the illustrations contribute a significantly to the nature of the narrative, presenting the reader with exactly the range of appearances, costumes and aspects of behaviour which are in the words. Tony Joseph has addressed this question, and his conclusion is one that I personally would support: he states that 'The fact that he did share in it is attested not only by the title page of the book itself, but by all the existing evidence, both written and oral alike." But Joseph adds that 'all the Punch payments were paid to George alone, indicating that, whatever part Weedon played thereafter, none of the text initially was his.'[226]

Looking at the book within the overall trajectory of George's writing as a whole, there is a clear sense of how and why it emerged organically, as a fulfilment of a life-long urge to write parodies, to assume a voice, as he always did as an actor and singer; Pooter is the natural progression from the fragments and snatches of other voices George had done over the years. Arguably, Pooter is an amalgam of a spectrum of different voices from social types which had been the target of the 'piano man's' humour for decades. If one asks questions on the literary pedigree of the book, looking at issues of intertextuality in the sense of where it came from, and what literary – as opposed to popular cultural – forms it has within it, then conclusions all depend on a number of glances at a sprinkling of sources. In a general application of character, Pooter stems from the ordinary diarists of the century such as farmers and servants who had written to reveal unknown life experience, with a quasi-documentary intention. More specifically, Pooter's voice is the confluence of the characters' voices in the sketches, songs and spoofs George had previously written or performed.

However, it is hard to erase the thought that there is a Dickensian quality to Pooter. Even his name is one that Dickens, ever careful to make his characters' names suited to personality and habits, would have conceived. George makes an effort to make all the names of the people in the book reach out into a Dickensian dimension, notably with Mr Murray Posh, who is indeed a quintessential *nouveau riche* person, and with the enigmatic pipe-smoking and silent Mr Padge, who we feel would have been perfect as a minor character in any Dickensian tale of blockish yet inscrutable bystanders to the main action.

The *Diary* has a quality of fiction at a time when cutting for pace and rapid narrative voice were not paramount; the reader goes at the pace Pooter wants, guided by the simple techniques of brief summaries before each chapter, short diary entries with short sentences included for maximum effect, and above all, the habit George has of giving the reader ample material for inference, rather than being told everything. The reader, in a sense, creates his or her own Pooter from the mould given.

As with so many books destined to become modern classics of their genre, the *Diary* did not attract much attention from reviewers at the time of its appearance. In most instances, it was simply listed among 'new publications' or 'new novels.' The 1890s saw a plethora of fiction from a publishing world in which small companies invested in fiction (as Arrowsmith had done) after having established lists of all varieties of non-fiction. Some publications gave a paragraph, as did *The Morning Post*, stating that it was 'humorous enough to satisfy the most exacting. The effect is heightened by an air of genuine simplicity ... it will surely provoke the laughter of the most morose.'[227]

Arrowsmith, in the throes of its massive production of fiction, produced a boxed list of announcements and listed quotes from reviews in its advertisements of the book. Mr Arrowsmith knew how to promote, writing: '*Saturday Review* speaks of Arrowsmith's Bristol Library as necessary to the traveller as a rug in winter and a dust-coat in summer.' The advertisement adds a quote from *The Sunday Sun*: 'We have read it from start to finish with the greatest enjoyment and many a hearty laugh, in the sun hard by a sandy beach.'[228]

The influence and impact of the *Diary* has been staggering. Edition has followed edition, and the book has initiated spin-off titles such as Keith Waterhouse's *The Collected Letters of a Nobody*, which consists of the kinds of letters Pooter would hypothetically have written in another context; this was followed by the same author's *Mrs Pooter's Diary* written in 1983. In discussions over the years about favourite recreational reading, it has figured prominently, as in several discussions in the press which have picked on Lord Rosebery's remark that 'I regard any bedroom I occupy as unfurnished without a copy of it. And that is an appreciation more sincere than any I could write.'[229] It has also been read on radio on several occasions and in 1954 it was produced for the stage by Basil Dean and performed at the Arts Theatre, Cambridge. George Benson and Dulcie Gray played the Pooters. Something about the title evokes responses and inspires, as is evidenced by a bizarre link with the autobiography of the Duchess of Bedford, born Nicole Milinaire, who called her autobiography, *Nicole Nobody* in 1974.

Finally, George would never have realised that his one novel was destined to be the kind of fiction that was at once a popular success and also rather a puzzle for academics when they strove to place the book in any particular genre. He would probably have sent up the whole situation in a satirical sketch.

8

THE END – AND THE INFLUENCE

'They have their exits and their entrances
And one man in his time plays many parts
Shakespeare: *As You Like It*

In the last years of the nineteenth century, George was involved in a series of return attempts to the stage, and each in its own way, the productions failed. There were lots of reasons why this was so. He was not well, and there is no doubt that his energy was at a low ebb, but there were also faults in the writing and the concepts of these works. The first, *His Majesty*, was a return to the Savoy: Burnand had done the libretto and Alexander Mackenzie wrote the music. Helen D'Oyly Carte was in control, and she could see that there were all kinds of difficulties. As Tony Joseph has pointed out, George's part of Ferdinand, King of Vingolia, was destined to fail, and his own lack of verve did not help: '... it was in essence a dull part ... The first night found him at his nervous worst. His old whimsicality, his former stage dominance, his rapport with the audience – all were lacking.'[230]

Then there was a venture with Weedon called *Young Mr Yarde*, a farce by Harold Ellis and Paul Rubens; this should have been a real hit, as it concerns a plot in which the aristocrat is impersonated by his valet. George and Weedon should have been in their element in this, but it had a very short run and bad reviews.

Arguably worst of all was *The Gay Pretenders*, at the Globe in 1900, based on the careers of the claimants to the throne in the late fifteenth century, Perkin Warbeck and Lambert Simnel. There was a very talented cast, including George's Savoy friend Richard Temple, and Letty Lind as Clothilde. But the reviewers saw it as a sad shadow of former glories, and something of a piece of rough work:

'... a bad specimen of semi-historical burlesque ... half
seriously treated and interesting as far as it goes ... eked
out by topical banalities in the way of allusions to current
matters and comic ditties that seem to have strayed out

of the reaches of musical comedy ... the result is by no means satisfactory ...' [231]

As Kurt Ganzl summed up: 'Grossmith's attempt to mix old burlesque with new methods and materials was not well enough done to justify itself.'[232]

Surely the fact that George did not appear at the end to take the curtain call for His Majesty is very significant. *The Referee* periodical commented that 'We cannot help thinking that he was not unwise in refraining from appearing before the curtain at the end of the performance.'[233] That must have gone down very hard with him, and arguably the experience was a major factor in George's steady decline afterwards. Slowly but inevitably, he became a marginal figure in terms of stage presence, returning to other things.

As usual, George kept on, after the turn of the new century, making appearances at charity and benefit events, such as the benefit for the magician Charles Bertram in April 1907, when he appeared to do his turn along with such luminaries as George Robey, Marie Tempest and Little Tich. He was also keen to reminisce, and typical of this was his tendency to write or talk about the great Sir Henry Irving, who was a friend of his for many years. He did still attempt some touring, but his energy was naturally not at the level it was formerly. There is an argument for opining that after so long a period of travelling and performing, the wearing out, the sheer overdone, overworked seam of his talent was thinning out and the sparkle was going.

However, there were still appearances at special events, some tours, and definitely the status of a celebrity to enjoy. He was so well-known that heads turned, people stopped to talk, and many wanted his autograph. His son GG was, by the early 1900s, also a rising star, having been established as one of George Edwardes' top rank actors at the Gaiety Theatre. As usual, George loved to share experiences which tended to highlight the absurdity of fame, and he was adept at finding fun in his 'image' – as in this snippet from his memories of encountering aspiring piano men: 'A young man called upon me to ask for my advice. He was short, pale, thin, wore pince-nez, and he was dreadfully plain. He said *I didn't sing well enough for the chorus, so I thought of going in for your sort of parts.*'[234]

In 1903 George was there at the famous closing performance of the great Gaiety Theatre (where his son GG had become a major star) and Irving was also there, having run across town to the theatre from Drury Lane where he was playing in *Dante*, an adaptation from a French play directed by his son, Laurence. A writer for *The Times* in 1961 in an article about his memory of meeting George, wrote about seeing both George and Irving on that momentous occasion. George played in an act from *The Toreador* alongside many others, and George wrote linking material for this show. The writer remembered Irving's arrival: 'I was rather proud of my description of the scene when Irving dashed across 'hot from hell' ... to join in the final tribute to Hollingshead [the manager of the Gaiety at one time]'[235]

Irving collapsed and died in the foyer of the Midland Hotel in Bradford in October 1905, and his manager, the novelist Bram Stoker, saw him die and had closed his eyes. Just a few months before that, George and Irving had a memorable encounter – an occasion in the footnotes of biography: B C Hilliam wrote about this in 1962, recalling the days when he was a cub reporter in Scarborough and snatched this remarkable coup. Irving was staying at the Prince of Wales hotel in Scarborough in mid-August 1905 when Hilliam called to write a piece for the local paper. He recalls that at just fifteen years old, he was given the brief: 'Sir Henry Irving is a dying man, but if you're admitted to his suite don't let on that you think so. In fact don't say anything at all to anybody. Just look and listen and get the day's bulletin from Mr Stoker.'[236]

When Hilliam arrived, there were five people in the room, including Stoker, and then there was another caller: he was 'leaning forward, his chain resting on hands cupped over the knob of an ebony walking stick, his eyes peering from behind pince-nez exactly as they were peering pictorially from so many Scarborough hoardings ... "Spa Theatre, Mr George Grossmith. For Six Matinees Only" – a dear old contemporary of Sir Henry's much admired and liked by him...'[237] George was asking for a favour – an appearance by the great man to boost his audience. Hilliam recalled George saying that he thought he was 'past it' and that he didn't know why business was so bad. George had some female performers working with him, a violinist, a singer and a pianist, and they were all called Dorothy, so Irving said, 'They don't like the idea of your three Dorothys.'

Irving made the guest appearance, to great applause and of course the theatre was packed. Hilliam concludes his memory with an account of George that night:

' … the house lights were dimmed and the curtain quickly raised, revealing Mr Grossmith's stool and piano in readiness. Considerately too, the old Savoyard got down to work without any special greeting or comment, but presently, in the midst of singing "the Happy Fatherland" – a skit on German exports … the words eluded him.'[238]

In that dilemma, apparently George exploited the situation, saying to Irving, 'You're making me nervous Sir, I really must ask you to leave!' It brought the house down.

George's love of mimicry was always likely to show itself, particularly where friends were concerned, and in his reminiscences of Irving, he told a story which illustrates just how close they were, and how much licence the great actor gave the 'clown.' The tale was that in Manchester once, Irving's carriage was waiting for him to arrive and a crowd gathered; George asked if the queue was waiting to see him, and was told that it was Irving they wanted. George thought the crowd would annoy the great man so he decided to do him 'a good turn' and he then wrote that he pulled up his collar, pulled down his Homburg hat, strutted across to the crowd with the gait of Irving himself, went into the carriage and they moved off, as did the crowd. Later, Irving came and found there was no crowd. George told him what had happened and Irving said, 'You ought not to have done that. I pay these people to come every night.' It may be apocryphal, but George liked to tell the story.[239]

Before retiring, one of the most significant dates in George's diary was the occasion when Gilbert was the guest at a Savoyard Celebration Dinner at the Hotel Cecil, marking the new season about to begin, with the *Yeomen of the Guard* as the first performance. At the dinner were George's old friends Barrington, Leonora Braham, Richard Temple and others, and in his speech, Gilbert naturally gave a prominent mention to George's part in the success of the comic operas which were by that time, established classics of the genre, repeatedly performed.[240]

In 1905 George's wife Rosa died, on 28 February, after a long illness. Their home at Dorset Square had been a wonderfully happy family centre – a place of great joy, fun and games. It is well attested that George was a father who liked to act like a child with the children on most occasions – joining in slides down the banister for instance; but he also had to be the father-figure as well, and in Victorian times that meant discipline. When Rosa died he must have looked back to those happy times, knowing just how much she had been his support, his closest friend, someone who shared his need for conviviality and the traffic of visitors and guests that both thrived on. As noted previously, with Rosa's particular guests often being Theosophists and spiritualists, it is highly likely that Dorset Square saw a séance very like the one George puts into the *Diary*, in which he also has a swipe at his friend Florence Marryat, who had published material on the paranormal: 'When I came home in the evening I found Carrie buried in a book on spiritualism, called *There is no Birth* by Florence Singleyet ... As she had not a word to say outside her book, I spent the rest of the evening altering the stair-carpets ...'[241] [Florence had published a book called *There is no Death*]

This hints at the amicable split in the Dorset Square home – George and his artistic friends against Rosa and her 'advanced' female circle, all clearly up-to-date with their interests in all kinds of science, both legitimate and fringe varieties. One has the feeling that this division was the focus for some friendly banter, and George surely put some of his affection for his wife into the ironical portrait of Carrie, whom Pooter deeply cares for, of course.

The family at Dorset Square had all grown up by the start of the new century when George was slowing down. The eldest, GG, was a notable star in his own right; Sylvia was born in 1875, Lawrence in 1877 and in 1880, Cordelia. By the time of their mother's death, Lawrence, who had begun his career as an engineer based in Bath, had taken to the stage in 1896 and followed the family tradition; the daughters had married, Sylvia to Stuart Bevan, and Cordelia to architect George Turner. If we need a confirmation of the closeness and warmth of the Grossmith family, one image says a great deal: a photo included in GG's autobiography which shows George and GG in deckchairs in a leafy garden, with GG's son George standing between the two men. George has written on the borders of the photo: 'The Three Georges!! I say! The middle George has cut us out as far as good looks are concerned?' The photo was taken in the year before George's death, and he sits, smiling and relaxed, having put on some weight, very much the happy grandfather.[242]

Tony Joseph, researching the first biography of George c1980 before its publication in 1983, was in touch with Grossmith descendants, and has written at length regarding the family holidays and the leisure time George had with them when not on tour. They took their holidays at Folkestone, or abroad in Europe, and then later at a vicarage at Goring-on-Thames. The most endearing aspect of George the family man is the way he carried on the traditions he had known, established by George the First, particularly the acting and indeed the writing of sketches, as had been done when he was a boy with the spoof of the last scene in *Hamlet*. The highlight in this respect was the Annual Juvenile Dance in which a play was written and performed and the adults (including Weedon) mixed with children in some riotous fun.

He was also writing again around 1908, working on the second volume of autobiography, *Piano and I*, which came out from Arrowsmith in 1910. It does not have the élan of the first volume, but is rather a chronicle of the piano entertainment, a mix of anecdote, scattered accounts of incidents on the move and also with illustrations, though not by Weedon but by Wallace Goldsmith.

In 1911 he lost someone else who had been important in his life: Gilbert. The writer's death was dramatic: he rescued a girl who was swimming in the lake at his grand country home, Grim's Dyke, and in the process his weak heart gave out.

George had always loved Folkestone. In 1901 he appeared there, invited by Burgiss Brown, and the *Folkestone Express* wrote in such a way that there is no doubt that he was held in very high esteem in that town:

> '... the public on Easter Monday evening were favoured with another opportunity of drinking at the fount of Grossmithian humour. Such is the magic magnetism of the great Savoyard's name that the Town Hall was packed and even a portion of the platform had to be requisitioned for seating purposes. Mr Grossmith was as droll as ever, and his witticism and humorous sallies kept the house in a ferment of merriment. Seldom has a Bank Holiday audience spent a more enjoyable two hours ...'[243]

There seems to be conflicting information as to when exactly George retired to Folkestone. The local paper, in his obituary, stated that 'Mr Grossmith lived in Folkestone for some four years ever since his retirement' so it is likely that he settled there in 1908, living at 32 Manor Road. He had earlier paid visits to the town to stay for long periods, at which time he stayed at a house in Millfield.

After retirement, he was perfectly happy to play a part in public events, and we have a glimpse of this in a long report of a 'Fancy Fair' at the Woodward Institute in January 1910. The Folkestone Dramatic and Music Club was formed in 1902, and it performed at the Institute. Three years after this Fair they became the Folkestone Operatic Society and performed at the Pleasure Gardens Theatre. The Fancy Fair was to raise funds, and George was the special guest, there to open proceedings. There were the usual side-shows and stalls, and the event raised almost £200 – perhaps close to £20,000 today. George enjoyed having a buttonhole flower presented to him by the little girl who was the 'fairy' at the show, and of course, it was expected that the Savoyard would give a speech, which was fully reported:

'He had known Folkestone for 35 years, and the more
he knew it, the more he loved it. If he could be of the
slightest use to them he would come and help them,
providing that he was not asleep in the afternoon. What
was so fascinating about bazaars was that it cost only 1s to
go in but it cost £10 to get out (Laughter). In declaring
the bazaar open, he could only put two little quotations
before them, "Buy, buy, buy" and as Rudyard Kipling
would say, "Pay, pay, pay" (applause).'[244]

The town was (and is) very attractive, with the Leas – an impressive open space prom – being arguably the most notable feature of the landscape. Victorian Folkestone was largely the product of a plan made by Decimus Burton for the Earl of Radnor in the 1840s; behind the prominent Leas area there are stucco-fronted residences, small hotels and guest houses that were there even in George's time. Burton had been busy across most of Kent, producing several churches including Holy Trinity in Tonbridge Wells, and also designing Holtwood House. He was taught and inspired by the great John Nash, and his work certainly contributed much to the image and special appeal of Folkestone. The railway was established there in 1843, so the visitors arrived in great numbers, intent on a relaxed family holiday. The mix of tranquillity and people-watching must have satisfied George as he enjoyed the views first when strolling around and then, later, pushed in his bath-chair.

The end came at two in the morning of 1 March 1912. The local obituary noted that he had been in declining health but that his death had come unexpectedly. He had been out in a bath-chair on his favourite area, the Leas. The obituary continued: 'On Wednesday Mr Grossmith rose as usual, but complained of feeling unwell, and very soon again he retired. From then he became gradually worse and died from syncope yesterday morning. He had been attended by Dr Streatfield.'[245] He would not have died of 'syncope' as that was merely another term for 'fainting' at the time, so a heart attack was the actual cause.

No doubt, as he was pushed around the Leas in his bath-chair, he thought of his old friend Toole, who had spent his last days in the same predicament, and had managed to joke to anyone who stopped to chat. George had been taken out, as the paper noted, as 'Up till recently it had been his custom to visit the promenade during the quieter part of almost every day.'[246]

On 11 May, George's will was reported in detail in *The Folkestone Herald*, and it contained one particularly telling sentence: £2,000 was left to GG from an estate valued at probate at £19, 257, and Weedon had been appointed executor. GG also had other strikingly important and valuable items, including 'the seal presented to him by Queen Victoria, two silver bowls presented to him by Sir William Gilbert' and an ivory baton he had used when GG had first appeared on the stage and George had conducted. Plenty of cash was left to several charities, and to the two daughters, £2,000 each. But this statement surely has a story behind it: 'to his son, Lawrence Grossmith, the Turkish crescent scarf pin presented to him by their majesties.' These pins, even when set with diamonds or garnets, are easily available today and at no great cost. Perhaps the one given by Victoria was of special status, or perhaps George knew that it would be not only an heirloom of great significance to the family, but might also become very valuable. Whatever the reasoning behind the inheritance, it seems small beer compared with the sums of £2,000 left to siblings. There is surely an unknown tale here, and we will probably never now the reason.

After such a long and distinguished career as a piano entertainer and patter singer, what was [247] the last solo Grossmith performance? It appears that *The Times* got it wrong, reporting that it was at the Hampstead Conservatoire in February 1906. The report of that event stated, '... for the future this veteran will appear only with others in the programme and them he will doubtless outshine ... His programme last night was one of great variety but in his imitation of his son at the Gaiety he was most successful.' [248]

But the actual final solo performance was in a Saturday matinee at Brighton on 7 November that same year. As Tony Joseph commented, the reporter at the time 'had no idea the occasion had any special significance' simply noting that ' the ravages of time apparently have no effect whatever on his genius for making people laugh … His sense of humour was undiminished …'[249]

The funeral was at Kensal Green cemetery on 5 March, the same location as that of his mother and father, and of his wife, Rosa. Along with family members there were several theatrical personalities present, including Beerbohm Tree, Squire Bancroft and Rutland Barrington.

Two days later, the auctioneers, Christies, held a sale of 'Spy' cartoons done by Leslie Ward: there was the one of George, alongside those of Victor Hugo, General Gordon, Gladstone and Garibaldi; George's picture cost the buyer twelve guineas. Surely he had now 'arrived' in posterity as well as in his own time, and was very definitely a 'Somebody.'

Somerset Maugham, writing in his notebook in 1901, reflected that 'In most biographies it is the subject's death which is most interesting. The last inevitable step has a fascination which no previous event can equal.'[250] This is particularly true in George's case, as we have an account of his home interior, in *The Idler* interview of 1893 with Raymond Blathwayt. The interview is mostly anecdotes, as were all interviews with him, and he was always evasive when it came to any other areas of life. What is interesting is that the piece contains a photograph of the study with dozens of framed pictures and prints around the walls and above the piano. George's will was later to list all these pictures and where they were to go: the will illuminates the interiority of a life that was almost always hidden at the expense of the persona promoted and presented to his 'public' (in every sense).

Naturally, biography has to end with something other than the report of a death, especially in this case. The Grossmith heritage ran through his actor sons, of course. GG was so famous at the time of his father's death that in 1913 there appeared Stanley Naylor's book, *Gaiety and George Grossmith*, which is arguably one of the first books written in terms of a celebrity culture on a grand scale: the sub-title is 'random reflections on the serious business of enjoyment' and at the core of Naylor's long profile of GG and his lifestyle is the notion of 'the art of savoir-vivre.'[251] The mainstream heritage was of course in GG's career, which had a meteoric rise. There is not much to go on if we look for details regarding the relationship between George and GG. GG devotes just a few pages (already referred to) in his autobiography, and there is an interesting mix of formality and familiarity in that relationship. George's place sat somewhere between professional adviser, playmate and Victorian paterfamilias. A fascinating scrap of insight is to be found in the letter George wrote to GG when the latter was twenty-one, in May 1895. George wrote, 'You are now your own master, and it is absolutely in your power to continue to return (as you always have done) the natural love which has been so freely and so willingly bestowed upon you by an incomparable mother and by an affectionate and admiring father.'[252]

By the early years of the new century, GG was such a success that his life and opinions, as Naylor's book shows, were representative of a fresh view of life, perhaps pitched mainly in terms of hedonism, but with a strong element of style, artistic flair and morality. The Grossmith sons were taking to the stage, as Irving's sons had, and GG gradually became a man with an image very much in contrast with his father. The several drawings of him taken from shows or from periodicals stress his height, with his long legs used in perspective to stress his elegance and style.

Following in his wake was Lawrence, and regardless of the point about George's will and the Turkish scarf pin, Lawrence carved out his own life on the stage (and on film) after a false start as an engineer. George had made sure that money was spent on schooling after his rise in income and his Savoy stardom: he had sent Lawrence to St Paul's College at Stony Stratford and then to Shrewsbury School, where one of the most notable graduates was the writer and war reporter, Henry Nevinson. Lawrence had had his theatrical debut in 1896 at the Court Theatre in *Mam'zelle Nitouche* by Herve, which had been premiered in 1883 in Paris. Later, his main stage career was in musical comedy in West End shows, and he was manager at the Savoy in 1913. Inevitably, he worked in cinema, and he appeared in such classics as *Tiger Bay* in 1934 and *Gaslight*, and he died in the year that came out, 1944.

There has been another kind of inheritance as well: the 'piano man' who had learned from John Orlando Parry had refashioned the piano-entertainer template, and he and Corney Grain became models for the next generation. In Edwardian Britain, the audience for all kinds of musical and theatrical entertainment expanded massively, and the London and provincial agencies wanted every kind of talent on their books and in their brochures, artistes who would cover the whole spectrum, from tenors and sopranos of classical pieces and oratorios, down to variety acts and quartets. A typical example is the company of Elston, based in Birkenhead: W H Elston, the proprietor referred to in my Introduction, had on his books several performers who were in the Grossmith mould, such as Nelson Jackson, described as 'Humorist, yarn teller, author and composer.' All Elston's artistes have black-and-white photos in their profiles, and lists of press recommendations.

Mr Leslie Harris, for instance, again described as 'humorist, pianist and raconteur' has a programme by the side of his photo. The picture shows him seated by his piano, with a smile upon his face and one hand reaching out in a welcoming gesture to his audience. The image derives from everything we have that describes George and Grain. He has watched and learned. Mr Elston's photographer obviously knew his business, as the whole image conveys happiness and fun.

His programme is:

PART 1
Pianoforte solo   Berlioz
Humorous skit upon the physical culture craze
Oh Mr Sandow   Harris
Recital   *The Midshipman*   Clement Scott
Humorous sketch   *My Wife's Afternoon*   Harris

PART 2
Pianoforte solo   Greig
Humorous interlude   Harris
Song   Harris
Half an hour with some modern entertainers
With illustrations from Corney Grain, George Grossmith, etc.
Concluding with:
Humorous musical sketch:
"Suburban Society"

That programme tells us so much about the impact and influence of George and Grain. The final sketch, though the text is unknown, gives a tantalising hint that somewhere behind the fun there is the spirit of Mr Pooter.

Even more directly a key part of the Edwardian musical entertainment stemming from George's work and personality is the story of Nellie Ganthony, who became known as 'The Female Grossmith.' Nellie was on Elston's books in his brochure of c1910 (the publication has no date). There she is described as offering 'humorous, musical and emotional sketches.' It is hard to ascertain what the last adjective refers to, of course, but Nellie was a hard worker, appearing from her first appearance in the mid-1890s in any kind of production she could find. In fact, she appeared on one occasion with George himself, near the start of her career. This was at the Birkbeck Institution in August 1898.

Nellie's work, when she appeared in music hall in 1900, was reviewed as 'touching on the lighter side of nature in a delineation of the peculiarities of buss passengers, during a pleasant quarter of an hour at the piano.'[253] She was at the King's Theatre, Hammersmith a few years later and the same journal wrote: 'A musical sketch gave rise to a lever de rideau entitled, The garden party which delighted everyone and recalled the best efforts of the late Mr Corney Grain.'[254] In the last years of the nineteenth century she made appearances as diverse as Mrs Horton in a short play, *The Kangaroo Girl*, at the Folkestone Pleasure Gardens, and sang at The Putney Creche. She was also elected to the board of the Actors' Association in 1897. She had learned form George and Corney that being seen was the main thing – as often as possible. She appeared in Marylebone to support the social work of the church, in 1898, contributing a sketch called The Bus Ride; in a revival of a farcical romance a few years later, she provided an opener and *The Times* noted that she gave a 'bright musical monologue.'[255]

The hard work and application paid off, and her star rose. Nellie later toured America, and the tag 'The Female Grossmith' was a very bright and workable commercial ploy. One comment in the press summed her up: 'She sings, she plays, she dances, and she does all with aplomb.'[256] She reached the popular status of the woman in the arts, successful and glamorous, who is asked By magazine editors for what we would now call 'soundbites' as in her 'little story' for 'The World of Women' for a local paper in 1900:

Miss Nellie Ganthony the well-known musical sketch entertainer, tells this Story of the servant question: "I was in the registry office the other day and overheard the following conversation between mistress and maid: Lady (exhausted) "Ah then, you are Kate. So glad you can come to me. I hope we shall understand each other. "Yes, mum." "I'm really very glad you are coming for you know it is quite difficult to get nice servants now." "Yes I know mum, for your class is coming down and mine is going up!"'[257]

Nellie, whose real name was Ada, married Toronto lawyer John Clark in April, 1898, and she appears to have ended her career soon after.

Nellie was not the only 'Female Grossmith.' There was also Fanny Wentworth, who was more specialised, being a music-hall star. In fact she was known for 'taking off' several music-hall stars as part of her act. She also appeared with Harry Osborne, doing 'the lad and lass from Ireland' Her big hit was *The Tin Gee-Gee*, written by Fred Cape. One report summed her up neatly: 'She is a brilliant pianiste and accomplished singer, and she has great powers of mimicry.'[258] She died in 1934.

George's influence was clearly massive: his style and his particular brand of versatility was destined to have an impact on younger, rising performers. Leon Berger's CD entitled *The Grossmith Legacy* has it just right: the kind of influence he had was the one that permeates a genre and a certain stage presence, something he shared with others of his peers in stage comedy, as he formed his own mannerisms and approaches to gentle satire throughout the 1860s to the end of the century.

There is in addition the question of the songs and sketches: essentially ephemeral art, these have mercifully been rescued from oblivion by Berger and Tillett in part, in the recordings previously described. There is also the treasure house of the *George Grossmith Birthday Book*, preserved and distributed by his daughters Cordelia and Sylvia. This appeared in 1904 with a dedication to 'Dear father: The compiling of this little book has been a great pleasure to us. It has not only reminded us of your later sketches, but it has recalled the songs you composed and sang to us when we were children.' In the sketch Castle Bang in particular, there is everything that went into the best dramatic humour, on a par with the surreal writing in similar works such as Dan *Leno: Hys Boke* in which Leno found a place to collect the shreds of playful whimsicality from his notebooks. In *Castle Bang* George lets loose all the originally childish *jeu d'esprit* of those family parties, with his detective, Bob Shocker, whose song 'How I Became a Detective' having some of the very best topical reference jokes in his repertoire. It follows the 'Modern Major General' patter rhythms of Gilbert and exploits the power of bathos to convey the sense of the surreal that George so loved, as in:

> 'A private detective I became, but ever since I've been one
> In spite of rogues and thieves at large, I've never even seen
> one.'

Summing up George Grossmith's life, a number of features come to the fore, with his sheer, determined application to work as the dominant one; this was integral to his commitment to the success and contentment of his family and their busy life together. From this work ethic and family-oriented mindset there came another strand, one that in many ways created his status and fame: the unique personality he had, surely a genetic acquirement. This was outgoing, confident and aware of the talent beneath the light social touch he conveyed of friendliness and fun. All the documentation on George's life indicates a character who had learned the value of thinking of the moment and contributing to the delight and pleasure inherent in that moment: something a natural clown does as naturally as breathing.

His small stature – some said his waspish or birdlike chirpiness and agility – puts him in the same genre of comedy as that which we think of when we watch Chaplin or Stan Laurel. Yet there was something else, and that relates to his social milieu. *Class* would not be the right word. He understood the fears, fads, preoccupations and obsessions of his age, but like all talented commentators on human folly, he understood and then transmuted human behaviour into the kind of humour we all share with ease and with understanding of the situation he 'sends up.' His age was one of parody, of the erosion of the Malvolio-like social front that an era of class consciousness generated. In our modern age of theory, applied everywhere, we might perhaps understand his humour as carnivalesque; but in the vocabulary of the Victorian age his essence was one of understanding and tolerance when it came to social foibles and follies. Like Swift, he saw his art as something based on the fact that he might dislike mankind but he loved Tom, Dick and Harry.

The last decades of Victoria's reign was one reinterpreted by writers and artists of all hues as something to be grasped through its distinctive voices: the monologue was everywhere, the singular voice coming through at a time when individualism was being rubbed out by the perfunctory actions of the masses; 'Nobody' in that context had to be given a voice, and Dickens had in some sense shown the way, as his reading tours had demonstrated. From Dickens's genius, it could be argued, came a multiplicity of individual voices, each claiming their selfhood in a world which effaced the monologue of consciousness and communal sharing. Without theory and through instinct, George Grossmith understood this and the response he felt was at the heart of his parodies and pastiches, his sketches and songs.

Origins and influences may be traced, but in the end, George Grossmith had a unique mix of a number of traits found in piano entertainers; he merely blended these with a very rare ability to convey his personality through innumerable voices from the fashions and cultures of his time.

In some ways, writing biography is like chasing ghosts and expecting them to be substantial, at the mercy of your pen and the resources of books and archives; yet somehow there is always a part of the subject's person and selfhood that remains in the shadows. I hope my efforts at chasing this particular ghost out into the light of historical imagination has at least partially succeeded.

9

Conclusions

*'I replied: 'Yes, Sir, I love my house and I love my
Neighbourhood and could not bear to leave it.'*
Pooter's Diary: *Chapter the Last*

George Grossmith will no doubt continue to be known in
the two spheres of literature and the stage; he will always
be associated with the first successes of Gilbert and Sullivan
and his Charles Pooter will continue to represent a special kind
of Englishness, notably from a period in which suburbia was fast
generating a set of values we often relate to the nature of being
English: the middle ground, routine, fear of extremes and the
cultivation of one's little domestic space. That George is known in
those two very contrasting areas of the arts is quite rare; comparison
might be made with and actor/writer but there is no doubt that
George's two outstanding productions – comic performance and
humorous prose – not only interfused in some ways, but also
gave enthusiasts for his life and work a sense of a probably unique
spectrum of genius, ranging from the solitary business of writing
to the light-hearted entertainment and socialising which seemed so
natural to him.

Posterity may never see him as anything more than this, but
arguably that would be fair. Assessments will always depend on the
evaluation of his humour: there is common ground in that, from which
everything in him sprang, from his conversation and whimsicality to
his ability to sing, write and act with a very closely defined readership
or audience in mind.

Accessing what might be called the inner man, the interiority of
the public person who was George Grossmith, has in some ways proved
to be a challenge: information is there, but in fragments and snippets
from a cluster of memoirs and in his own brief admissions in his own
autobiographical writings, such as the one paragraph he devotes to
his nervousness before performance. That is almost universal in those
who live to entertain, of course, but the inner churnings of doubts

129

and excitement he must have experienced when going from penny readings entertainer to major opera star can only be surmised.

He is, in general terms, far more remembered for his one modern classic with Weedon, and perhaps more general readers respond to the word 'Pooter' than they do to 'Grossmith.' But in theatre history, the historian is repeatedly struck (and often deeply affected by) the oblivion awaiting stars who trod the boards and whose promotional pictures were displayed in every tobacconist shop. As I write this in early 2013, announcements in the press have been made about the availability for family historians of new criminal records, and one feature story concerns Florence Leslie, an attractive and popular West End actress who was ruined by drink, first standing before the magistrates at the age of just 22; her destiny was to be listed among the 'habitual drunkards' and was at one point placed in a 'certified inebriate reformatory.' The woman who was loved and applauded by thousands was destined to be number 2042 in the habitual drunkards logbook kept by the police. Her only friends would be the Christian police court missionaries.

At least George had a quiet and dignified exit in his retirement location by the sea, and his namesake son on the stage to carry on the family image, but it makes an interesting contrast to note that GG had a whole (and rather hagiographical) volume on his life and stage personality in print, whereas George had no more than a heap of ephemeral press reviews and forgotten theatre programmes in the imaginary personal file.

Grossmith the writer has, paradoxically, taken first place in terms of today's situation with regard to his standing and impact. His one work of fiction continues to be reprinted (with Weedon rather in the background) and it has generated a number of spin-offs, but the principal inheritance we have from this is its provision of a template for a certain inextinguishable version of Englishness – that in the small-scale suburban bliss so many of us aspire to, for comfort and security at least. Deeply positioned within that template we have the notion of self-importance and a profound fear of being too brash, too noticed, too often observed and commented on. Yet, in a strange way, Pooter is also a kind of reluctant performer, almost shadowing the need of his creator to entertain, be seen, command attention.

On the credit side, in terms of posterity at least, there has been a certain amount of attention paid to *The Diary of a Nobody* and its importance, as well as its sheer humorous, quirky quality, as George's sense of humour and the total lightness of his attitude to life were transmuted from stage to print. Having looked closely at Grossmith's career as a comic pianist and singer, we can surely place him, along with John Parry, as one of the very first of that breed, with Ivor Novello, Noel Coward and then perhaps some jazz performers such as Blossom Dearie continuing that genre. As discussed in Chapter Five, arguably, Charles Dibdin was father of them all, but George had a definite originality. What George did, partly learned from Parry but with his own original additions, was to use a mix of comic methods, integrated into a narrative, as in his patter songs.

In contrast, if we try to assess the Grossmith impact on how Gilbert and Sullivan's works have been staged and conceived since his death, there is no doubt that George's imprint is always there, to be either challenged and changed or merely reproduced. The Savoy operas are a perfect example of the stage genre which has a dual afterlife, that is, in the time following the first, classical and template productions. This means that the director may give the audience of Savoyard enthusiasts what they want, with the Grossmith roles being done as they were by the man himself, or to experiment. Generally, the Grossmith performance dominates, but that is not to say that the best directors and performers today don't lose the real sparkle and panache of the patter roles.

In this respect, the Grossmith legacy on the stage is being preserved most notably by Simon Butteriss, a singer, writer and performer who has a special interest in George's life and work, and who has written and performed *A Salaried Wit*. This is a film concerned with George's work with Gilbert and Sullivan. The image we have here is of George very much in the role of jester, with the pressures of making sure that his comedy nurtures not only a response from the audience, but an interplay of affection as well. Simon Butteriss, in an interview, opined that 'George Grossmith probably did more in the cause of forcing opera singers to act than anyone else in the whole history of opera.'

If we want to imagine what George Grossmith would have been like – how he moved, used his body and created a rapport with his audience – the closest we will get to that experience which the Savoy crowds had in the 1880s would be to watch Simon Butteriss perform the Grossmith roles. Simon directs the works as well, and it is clear from so many of his performances that he pays close attention to every nuance in the actions and words which interweave to create the special humour of a Gilbert and Sullivan musical opera as it was meant to be.

*

Purely in terms of Grossmith the writer, then one can only express amazement that critical discussion of the *Diary* has been so peripheral. In the most extensive study of the literature of the late Victorian and Edwardian suburbs, Lynne Hapgood's *Margins of Desire* (see bibliography) the book is allotted just two pages. There is something elusive about the novel, created no doubt by its uneasy status within conceptions of fictional form generally, and this is compounded by its slippery tendency in any attempt to define or compartmentalise it. It is difficult to escape the fact that the book was written by a man with origins, influence and attitudes far away from any mainstream literary man aiming to establish a reputation as a novelist.

We are left with the customary problem of the biographer: the elusive nature of the subject. Biographical enquiry inevitably has to take in both the dominant and the secondary narratives around any given life. In Grossmith's case, even his own two memoirs deal so much with his professional life as an entertainer that it is easy to lose the man himself. He never liked soul-searching and was too much turned to the light rather than to the darker, less palpable elements in life.

His classic work of fiction stands alone, in some respects a curiosity, and in other ways an item in a specific genre of fiction which has been produced by people with other mainstream careers. But is it to be recalled that fundamentally, Grossmith was a writer of comedy with a very documentary, topical touch, no doubt fed by his early phase as a Bow Street reporter, when the comedy had to be suppressed, but the documentation with people at the heart of the story was still the strongest element.

In the 1880s and 1890s, there were comments on 'the new humour' as there were on almost everything connected with entertaining writing aimed at an audience which would have included the younger generation of working and lower middle class people, mainly men, clerking and pen-pushing in the new towns. Jerome K Jerome's *Three Men in a Boat* had appealed to that readership, and it is possible to see similarities between Grossmith and Jerome. They were both published by Arrowsmith, and there is some significance in that, but on the whole the 'new humour' was one defined by a sense in the writing devices and narrative strategies that there was no weight of literary and cultural knowledge required other than the intensely contemporary. Both books (and much of the new journalism in the better, more aspirational periodicals) cultivated that style and content. It was a good read, free from any burden of extra-textual demands on one's educational acquisitions. Arguably, there was something of Charles Lamb behind it all – a style of writing direct, lucid and democratic. That bunch of adjectives would have pleased both Pooter and George, one feels.

Grossmith may remain something of a loose cannon in terms of attempts to place and define his achievements in all spheres of activity, but on the whole his position of importance in Gilbert and Sullivan research and in Victorian humorous writing is most definitely assured. It is to be hoped that as time goes on, more interest is taken in not only his life but in the Grossmith dynasty, which perhaps still awaits its historian and biographer. Regarding George's own life, there will always be that slightly occluded element, something intensely private: the rest is highly visible, as befits a performer and unstoppable joker, and he only wanted to be remembered as the Society Clown – something he made his own speciality. It was always morphing into the Domestic Clown and the Club Clown, but all this lightness was of a piece, and integral to the man.

Acknowledgements

Sources of information for this project have sometimes given me the feeling that, like many crime novels, the best way to work was to go backwards. So much was said on reflection about George Grossmith that part of the biography is like a process of facial reconstruction, projecting probable features from known basic material. For this reason, assembling the jigsaw of his later life in particular has meant that an assembly of fragmentary material has been essential. As my last pages show, this has also entailed a certain amount of empathic imagining based on places and things. Most biographers would probably agree that this element is the most satisfying of all the stylistic ploys at our disposal.

Many people have helped with the searches into libraries and archives here. Special thanks go to Karen Morgan, Head Librarian and archivist at the North London Collegiate School, for help in tracing material on Grossmith's schooling. For other material, thanks to Alexa Rees at Nottinghamshire Archives and to staff at Shropshire Archives. For some of the sources on dramatic material, the staff at the Hull History Centre and at the University of Hull were very helpful. For help with material from the Mander and Michenson collection, thanks go to Heather Romaine and Jill Sullivan.

In literary criticism and history, very helpful work has been done by Peter Morton, whose website (see below in the bibliography) is extremely informative. The same thanks are due to Boise State University for texts and materials relating to Gilbert and Sullivan at their web site (again, listed below).

For John Parry, and for permission to use the pictures of him in this book, thanks go to Janet Snowman, curator of art and iconography at the Royal College of Music, who has been a wonderful contact and a great help in the research. Also, Margaret Jones at the University of Cambridge library was very helpful.

Similarly, thanks go to the biographer of W S Gilbert, Andrew Crowther, for the use of the portrait of Gilbert, and for his general help with research. I also have to thank Mr Wilfrid de Freitas for his help in some detective work.

Grossmith's last years in Folkestone have been hard to probe,

134

but thanks go to Jan-Christine Johnson (see below) for help with following up leads from her original article on those last years, and also Alan Taylor, of the Folkestone Local History Society, helped with that research, supplying the photograph of Grossmith's home there. Also, at Folkestone Library, Andrew Hudson was very helpful in locating materials on Grossmith's last years in the town, providing materials from the local newspaper archive of *The Folkestone Herald* and *The Folkestone Express.*

For modern performance, I am indebted to Simon Butteriss, singer, actor and director, who has studied Grossmith in considerable depth as a 'patter man.' Simon directs Gilbert and Sullivan, and has a special interest in performing the Savoy Grossmith roles. His film, *A Salaried Wit*, Capriol Films, 2006) describes Grossmith the Savoyard and offers valuable insights into his performances. The film was directed and produced by Tony Britten.

The Music and Lyrics:
One thing we will never know for sure is what a Grossmith piano performance was like, at least with documentary accuracy: but Leon Berger and others have helped to give us something very close to what the real things must have been like.
Leon Berger is the most well-known performer and interpreter of the Grossmith canon in this context; he had been most helpful in pointing me towards related material, and his recordings have given special insights into the Grossmith songbook; the words on the page are transmuted into life by the voice. Anyone wishing to experience Berger's recordings should consult:
The Grossmith Legacy (Berger and Selwyn Tillett :Diversions, 2006)
Society Clown: The Songs of George Grossmith (Leon Berger: Orchard, 2000)
To my knowledge, there is no other realisation of the Grossmith canon of songs available.

BIBLIOGRAPHY AND SOURCES

Note:

As with so many literary and theatrical figures from this period, much of the source material is scattered in biographies, ephemera, letters and diaries. George Grossmith is no exception, and the same applies yet more acutely in the case of his father, George the First, who travelled and lectured wherever and whenever he could. We are more fortunate with the writings of GG, as he wrote an autobiography of more substance than his father's, whose two volumes require a deal of expansion and context. Yet even GG's book is slight on the topic of his father. The result has been a determined but very rewarding trawl through a mass of print, and along the way there have been those fascinating insights, discovered through sheer serendipity, in such places as local papers and interviews. But as a foundation for all this, Tony Joseph's book has led the way to all Grossmithians who have followed and who are under the spell of the 'Society Clown.'

In terms of original documents, Tony Joseph, in his 1982 biography, had contact with Grossmith descendants and easy access to letter collections. Thankfully, his work on this has meant that it has not been necessary to search out information from these sources, now held, at least in part, at The National Archives. But other manuscript sources have been located and used, scattered across archives in various record offices across the land.

It may also be noted that I have filled out the story of George the First from Tony Joseph's account, as material relating to his numerous areas of work is now easier to find: this includes sources are varied as appearances at mechanics' institutes and Masonic halls, and from penny readings to local theatres.

Primary Sources

Books

Note:

In editions cited, the date of first publication is given in brackets. The works cited are those editions used with regard to my text.

Within the book, citations from *The Diary of a Nobody* are from the edition edited by Ed Glinert (London: Penguin, 1999)

Works by George/George and Weedon Grossmith / George Grossmith the Younger

Note: Although the first George Grossmith (George the First) published nothing, GG (known as Junior, and who died in 1935) published also.

Bevan, Sylvia Grossmith, and Grossmith, Cordelia, *The George Grossmith Birthday Book*
This was compiled in 1904 by Grossmith's two daughters. The text, edited by David Trutt, is available at www.haddon-hall.com/GilbertBooks/GeorgeGrossmithBirthdayBook.html
Grossmith, George, *A Society Clown* (1888) Text used: Memphis: General Books, 2012
Grossmith, George, *Piano and I: Further Reminiscences* (1910)
Grossmith, George and Weedon, *The Diary of a Nobody* (Bristol: Arrowsmith, 1892) (London:Penguin, 1999)
Grossmith, George (Jnr.) *G.G.* (London:Hutchinson, 1933)
Grossmith, Weedon, *From Studio to Stage* (London: John Lane, 1913)

Essays and introductions in Editions of *The Diary of a Nobody*

Glinert, Ed, *Introduction to The Diary of a Nobody* (London: Penguin, 1999)
This is particularly useful for the London context, as Ed Glinert is a renowned expert on the city's history.
Flint, Kate (Ed) Introduction: *The Diary of a Nobody* (Oxford: OUP, 2008)
Kate Flint has made a close study of late Victorian suburbia, and her essay here places the book in that specific context.
Morton, Peter, Introduction: *The Diary of a Nobody* (Peterborough, Ontario: Broadview, 2008)
Note: Peter Morton also has much valuable material on Grossmith and his literary context on his web site at: https://sites.google.com/petermorton's website

Contemporary Works on or including Grossmith

Anon. 'The Society Clown at Home' *The Graphic* June 26, 1890
Barrington, Rutland, *More Rutland Barrington, By Himself* (London:Grant Richards, 1911)

Blathwayt, Raymond, 'Lions in their Dens- George Grossmith and the Humour of him'
The Idler 1893 pp. 68-81

Bond, Jessie, *The Life and Reminiscences of Jessie Bond* (London: Macmillan, 1930) Included on the web site of the Boise State Gilbert and Sullivan Archive, to which text my references relate.

Grain, Corney, *Corney Grain By Himself* (London: John Murray, 1858)

Hutchinson, Horace G., *Portraits of the Eighties* (London: Fisher Unwin, 1920)

Marryat, Florence, *Tom Tiddler's Ground* (London: Sonnenschein, Lowrey & Co, 1886)

Morton, William, *I Remember: A Feat of Memory* (Hull: Goddard, Walker, 1934)

Naylor, Stanley, *Gaiety and George Grossmith* (London: Stanley Paul, 1913)

Soldene, Emily, *My Theatrical and Musical Recollections* (London: Downey & Co, 1897)

Manuscripts

Grain, Corney, Letter to Mrs Robertson December 27 1889
Grossmith, Weedon, Letter to Mrs Tweedie May 29 1894
(author's collection)

Other Works

Anon. *Mr Punch in Wig and Gown* (London: Educational Books Co., 1910)

Archer, Frank, *An Actor's Notebooks* (London: Stanley Paul, 1910)

Archer, William, *Real Conversations* (London: William Heinemann, 1904)

Bennett, Arnold, *The Journals* (Ed. Frank Swinnerton) (London: Penguin, 1954)

Bonham-Carter, Victor, *Authors by Profession* (London: The Society of Authors, 1978)

Carpenter, J E, *Penny Readings in Prose and Verse* (London: Frederick Warne, 1870)

Church, Richard, *The Voyage Home* (London: Heinemann, 1964)

Cook, Clarence, *The House Beautiful: an essay on beds, tables, stools and candlesticks* (New York: Scribner, 1878)

Day, W C, *Behind the Footlights* (London: Frederick Warne, 1885)

Dickens, Charles, *My Early Times* Edited by Peter Rowland (London: Aurum Press, 1988)

Dickens, Charles, *Oliver Twist* (1837-38) (London: Hazell, Watson and Viney, 1926)

Furniss, Harry, *My Bohemian Days* (London: Hurst and Blackett, 1919)

Greville, Charles, *The Diaries of Charles Greville* Edited by Edward Pearce (London: Pimlico, 2006)

Haining, Peter (Ed), *Hunted Down: The Detective Stories of Charles Dickens* (London: Peter Owen, 2006)

Hawkins, Sir Henry *The Reminiscences* (London: Nelson and sons,1904)

Howse, Christopher (Ed) *How We Saw It* (London: Daily Telegraph, 2005)

Gilbert, W S, *Eight Original Comic Operas* (London: Chappell, 1895)

Gilbert, W S, *The Bab Ballads* (London: Macmillan, 1924)

Gilbert, W S, *The Savoy Operas* (Various dates) (Oxford: Oxford University Press, 2 vols 1962)

Mander, Raymond and Mitchenson, Joe, *Victorian and Edwardian Entertainment From Old Photographs* (London: Batsford, 1978)

Maugham, Somerset, *A Writer's Notebook* (London: Heinemann, 1949)

Naylor, Stanley, *Gaiety and George Grossmith* (London: Stanley Paul, 1913)

Nelson, Alexander Abercromby, *Report of the Proceedings at Bow Street Police Court on the Committal of Colonel Nelson and Lieutenant Brand for the murder of Mr G W Gordon* (1867) reprinted by Cornell University Library 2010)

Pascoe, Charles Eyre, *The Dramatic List: a record of the principal performances of living actors* (London: William Clowes, 1879)

Pemberton, Max, *Sixty years Ago and After* (London: Hutchinson, 1936)

Reynolds, Ada M, *The Life and Work of Frank Holl* (London: Methuen, 1912)

Rhodes, William Barnes, *Bombastes Furioso* (1810) (London: Bell and Daldy, 1873)

Rolph, C H, *London Particulars* (Oxford: Oxford University Press, 1980)

Sala, George Augustus, *Twice Round the Clock, or the hours of the day and night in London* (London: Martin, 1858)

Scott, Clement, *The Theatre Annual* (London: The Stage Office, 1888)

Strachey, Lytton, 'Lancaster gate' in Holroyd, Michael and Levy, Paul, *The Shorter Strachey* (OUP, 1980) pp. 1-13

Tennyson, Alfred, *The Works of Alfred, Lord Tennyson* (London: Macmillan, 1895) *The Stage Cyclopaedia* (London: The Stage, 1909)

Thorne, George, *Jots* (Bristol: Arrowsmith, 1897)

Toole, J L, *Reminiscences of J L Toole* (London: Hurst and Blackett, 1889)

Ward Lock Illustrated Guides; Folkestone (Ward Lock, 1930)

Wellesley, Victor, *Recollections of a Soldier-Diplomat* (London: Hutchinson

Wilder, Marshall P, *The People I've Smiled With: recollections of a merry little Life* (New York: O M Dunham, 1886)

Williams, Montagu, *Leaves of a Life* (London: Macmillan, 1890)

Williamson (Ed) *The German Reeds and Corney Grain: records and reminiscences* (London: A D Innes, 1985)

Periodicals/Reference
'Mr George Grossmith' *Folkestone Herald* March 2, 1912

'Mr George Grossmith at Folkestone' *Folkestone Express* April 13, 1901 *Illustrated London News Supplement* (January, 1864)

Robbins, Alfred, 'Masonic Benevolence' *The Quiver* 1903 pp.676-680

Wisden Almanac 1913

'Woodward Institute' *Folkestone Herald* January 29 1910

Ephemera
List of Artistes Brochure produced by the Premier Provincial Entertainment and Concert Bureau, Birkenhead (no date: c1910) W H Elston, director, and printed by Brimmell's, Birkenhead. This includes a profile of Nellie Ganthony.

Secondary Sources

Books

Agate, James, *Agate's Folly* (London: Chapman and Hall, 1925)

Agate, James, *Buzz! Buzz! Essays of the Theatre* (London: W. Collins, 1917)

Agate, James, *Ego, The Autobiography of James Agate* Vol. 1 (London: Hamish Hamilton, 1935)

Agate, James, *Ego 9* (London: George Harrap, 1939)

Agate, James, *Those Were the Nights* (London: Hutchinson, 1946)

Baily, Leslie, *The Gilbert and Sullivan Book* (London: Cassell, 1952)

Bailey, Peter, *Popular Culture and Performance in the Victorian City*

Bailey, Peter, (Ed) *Music Hall: The Business of Pleasure* (Milton Keynes: Open University, 1986)   (Cambridge: CUP, 1998)

Bevan, Ian, *Royal Performance* (London: Hutchinson, 1954)

Birkett, Jeremy and Richardson, John, *Lillie Langtry* (Poole: Blandford Press, 1979)

Blake, Robert, *D'Israeli* (London: Eyre and Spottiswoode, 1966)

Bloom, Ursula, *Curtain Call for the Guv'nor* (London: Hutchinson, 1954)

Bott, Alan, *Our Fathers* (London: Heinemann, 1902)

Bryson, Bill, *At Home* (London: Transworld, 2010)

Charles, Barrie, *Kill the Queen: the eight assassination attempts on Queen Victoria* (Stroud: Amberley, 2012)

Childs, W M, *The Town of Reading During the Early Part of the Nineteenth Century* (Reading: University College, 1910)

Crowther, Andrew, *Gilbert of Gilbert and Sullivan* (Stroud: History Press, 2011)

Delany, Paul, *George Gissing* (London: Pimlico, 2008)

Dutton, Ralph, *The Victorian Home* (London: Batsford, 1954)

Fatant, Paul, *Mark Twain Speaking* (Iowa City: University of Iowa Press, 1976)

Gillett, Paula, *Musical Women in England 1870-1914* (Basingstoke: Palgrave Macmillan, 2000)

Ellmann, Richard, *Oscar Wilde* (London: Hamish Hamilton, 1989)

Ganzl, Kurt, *The British Musical Theatre Vol.1 1865-1914* (London: Macmillan, 1986)

Gillett, Paula, *The Victorian Painter's World* (Stroud: Sutton, 1990)

Gammond, Peter, *Offenbach* (London: Omnibus Press, 1980)

Green, Benny, *The Last Empires* (London: Pavilion, 1986)

Green, Roger Lancelyn, *A E W Mason* (London: Max Parrish, 1952)

Hapgood, Lynne, *Margins of Desire: The suburbs in fiction and culture 1880-1925* (Manchester: Manchester University Press, 2005

Harrison, J F C, *Learning and Living 1790-1960: a study in the history of the English adult education movement* (London: Routledge and Kegan Paul, 1961)

Hastings, Selina, *The Secret Lives of Somerset Maugham* (London: John Murray, 2009)

Holroyd, Michael, *Bernard Shaw* (London: Vintage, 1998)

Hughes, Gervase, *Composers of Operetta* (London: Macmillan, 1962)

Inwood, Stephen, *City of Cities: The Birth of Modern London* (London: Macmillan, 2005)

Jackson, Lee, *A Dictionary of Victorian London* (London: Anthem Press, 2006)

Joseph, Tony, *George Grossmith, Biography of a Savoyard* (Bristol: Bunthorne Books, 1982)

Kilgarriff, Michael, *Grace, Beauty and Banjos: peculiar lives and strange times of music
hall artistes and variety artistes* (London: Oberon Books, 1998)

Kilgarriff, Michael, *The Golden Age of Melodrama* (London: Wolfe Publishing, 1974)

Lancaster, Osbert, *Homes Sweet Homes* (London: John Murray, 1939)

Lehmann, Joseph *All Sir Garnet: A life of Field-Marshall Lord Wolseley* (London:Jonathan Cape, 1964)

Longford, Elizabeth, *Victoria R.I.* (London: Weidenfeld & Nicolson, 1964)

Luckhurst, Mary & Moody, Jane, (Eds) *Theatre and Celebrity in Britain 1660-2000* (Houndmills: Palgrave Macmillan, 2005)

MacQueen-Pope, Walter, *Carriages at Eleven: The Story of the Edwardian Theatre* (London: Robert Hale, 1972)

Maunder, Andrew, *Varieties of Women's Sensational Fiction 1855-1890* (London: Pickering and Chatto, 2004)

Middlemas, Robert Keith, *The Master Builders* (London: Hutchinson, 1963)

Mitchell, R J and Leys, M D R, *A History of London Life* (London: Penguin, 1958)

Morris, Donald R, *The Washing of the Spears* (London: Jonathan Cape, 1965)

Negev, Eilat, and Koren, Yehuda, *The First Lady of Fleet Street* (London: The Robson Press, 2012)

Oulton, Carolyn W de la, *Below the Fairy City* (Brighton: Victorian Secrets, 2012)

Page, William, *The Victoria County History of the Counties of England: Kent* Vol III (London: Constable, 1926)

Palmer, Beth, *Florence Marryat on Page and Stage* (Oxford: OUP, 2011)

Palmer, Beth, 'Florence Marryat on Page and on Stage' *Oxford Scholarship Online* 2012

Pearson, Hesketh, *Edward VII* (Houndmills: Palgrave Macmillan, 2007)

Phillips, Lawrence, *A Mighty Mass of Brick and Smoke: Victorian and Edwardian*

Representations of London (Amsterdam: Editions Rodopi, 2007)

Picard, Liza, *Victorian London* (London: Phoenix, 2005)

Power, Sally, et alia, *Education and the Middle Class* (Milton Keynes: Open University, 2003)

Quennell, Peter, *Victorian Panorama* (London: Batsford, 1937)

Scott, Harold, *The Early Doors* (Wakefield: EP Publishing, 1977)

Scott, Patrick and Fletcher, Pauline, *Culture and Education in Victorian Britain* (London: Associated University Presses, 1984)

Sherston, Erroll, *London's Lost Theatres of the Nineteenth Century* (London: John Lane, 1925)

Snowman, Janet, *John Orlando Parry and the Theatre of London* (London: The author, 2010)

Tindall, Gillian, *Three Houses, Many Lives* (London: Vintage, 2013)

Tomalin, Claire, *Charles Dickens: A Life* (London: Penguin, 2011)

Traubner, Richard, *Operetta: A Theatrical History* (Oxford: Routledge, 2003)

Trewin, J C, *Theatre Bedside Book* (London: David & Charles, 1974)

Vincent, Adrian, *A Companion to Victorian and Edwardian Artists* (Newton Abbot: David & Charles, 1991)

Wild, Jonathan, *The Rise of the Office Clerk in Literary Culture 1880-1939* (Basingstoke: Palgrave Macmillan, 2006)

Wilkinson, Penny, *That's Entertainment* (Hull: Hull City Museums, 1989)

Wood, J Hickory, *Dan Leno* (London: Methuen, 1905)

Articles/Essays

Anon. 'The Last Night of the First Gaiety' *The Times* July 12, 1961 p.12

Anon. 'The Stage as a Profession: an 1897 Controversy' *The Shaw Review* Vol. 11 No. 2 May, 1968 pp.52-78

Bailey, Peter, 'White Collars, Grey Lives? The Lower Middle Class Revisited' *Journal of British Studies* Vol. 38 No 3 pp.273-290

Byerly, Alison, 'From Schoolroom to Stage: Reading Aloud and the Domestication of Victorian Theatre (see Scott and Fletcher, above, pp.125-141)

Donald, Moira, Tranquil Havens? Critiquing the idea of home as the middle class Sanctuary' in Bryden, Inga & Floyd, Janet, (Eds.) *Domestic Space* (Manchester: Manchester University Press, 1999) pp.103-120

Hammerton, A.James, 'Pooterism or Partnership? Marriage & Masculine Identity In the Lower Middle Class 1870-1920' *Journal of British Studies* Vol. 38 No. 3

Johnson, Jan-Christine, 'Discovering George Grossmith in Folkestone' *The Gaiety* (Spring 2005) pp.37-43

Jones, Sarah Olwen, 'Staging the Interior: The Public and Private Intimacies of Thomas And Jane Carlyle's Domestic Lives' *Journal of Victorian Culture* Vol.18, No.2 pp.181-197

Kent, Christopher, 'The Whittington Club: A Bohemian Experiment in Middle Class Sexual Reform' *Victorian Studies* Vol. 18 No. 1 September 1974 pp.31-55

Milne-Smith, Amy, 'A Flight to Domesticity? Making a Home in the Gentlemen's

Clubs of London 1880-1914' Journal of British Studies Vol. 45 No. 4 October 2006 pp.796-818

Prescott, Andrew, 'Brother Irving: Sir Henry Irving and Freemasonry' see the Society journal. The text is online at www.theirvingsociety.org.uk/brother_irving.htm

Squire, J C., *Introduction* to 1924 edition of *The Diary of a Nobody* (see above)

Stedman, Jane W., 'General Utility: Victorian Author-Actors from Knowles to Pinero' *Educational Theatre Journal* Vol. 24 No. 3 October 1972 pp.289-301

White, Jerry, 'On Stinkomalee' *Times Literary Supplement* December 14 2012 pp.14-15

Archives
The Gilbert and Sullivan Archive, Boise State University
The Mander and Michenson collection, University of Bristol
    Department of Theatre Nottinghamshire Archives: letters of
    George Grossmith (Senior) to the secretary of the Newark
    Institution, 1858-1863 Ref: DD/1440

Periodicals Consulted
The Daily Graphic
The Era
The Idler
The Pall Mall Gazette
The Quiver
The Sketch
The Stage
The Strand Magazine

Non-Book Digital
British Library Nineteenth Century Newspapers
The Times Digital Archive

Websites
www.british-history.ac.uk
www.diamond.boisestate.edu/gas/
www.folkestonehistory.org/
www.florencemarryat.org/
www.google.com/site/petermortonswebsite
www.haddon-hall.com/GilbertBooks/
    GeorgeGrossmithBirthdayBook.html
www.japansociety.org.uk
www.victorianturkishbath.org/6directory (Malcolm Shifrin's site for
    the exchange
of information on Turkish baths.)

Blogs
Eugene Byrne: Called Back (on Arrowsmith publishers) see: www.
    eugenebyrne.wordpress.com/2011/01/16/called-back-1883/
Susi Woodhouse: *John Orlando Parry* at MusiCB3 Blog (University
    Library, Cambridge)

ENDNOTES

1   DOAN p.125
2   E M Forster, *Howard's End* p.101
3   Max Wall, *The Fool on the Hill* p.17
4   Col. Frederick Wellesley, *Recollections of a Soldier-Diplomat* p.73
5   Richard Findlater, *Lilian Baylis: The Lady of the Old Vic* p.48
6   See *The Daily Graphic* June 12 1890 p.5
7   This is part of promotional material in Elston's *List of Artistes* p.9
8   See 'The Society Clown at Home' *The Daily Graphic* June 26 1890 p.10
9   See Ursula Bloom, *Curtain Call for the Guv'nor* pp.51-54
10 ASC p.2
11 The Collegiate School for Boys appears to have been inspired by Miss Buss's school. Dale was prominent in the whole context of church education in London at the time. He was in fact a patron of Miss Buss's school.
12 In ASC George stresses the illicit nature of his love for boxing. His father would have preferred less aggressive hobbies. But he was at times dictatorial, in spite of his love of fun.
13 J E Carpenter, *Penny Readings in Prose and Verse* p.1
14 Ibid. p.1
15 Alison Byerley, ' From Schoolroom to Stage: Reading Aloud and the Domestication of Victorian Theatre' in Scott and Fletcher p.131
16 Quoted in Joseph, p.22
17 Child, W M *The Town of Reading During the Early Part of the Nineteenth Century* p.74
18 Ibid. p.77
19 Ibid. p.75
20 Mitchell, R J and Leys, M D R., *A History of London Life* p.316
21 See Thornbury, *Old and New London*
22 See *The Leeds Mercury* August 5 1843 p.5
23 Weedon Grossmith, *From Studio to Stage* p.2
24 J E Carpenter, *Penny Readings in Prose and Verse* p.5
25 William Morton, *I Remember* p.42
26 Ibid. p.119
27 Ibid. p.119
28 ASC p.1
29 Ibid. p.1
30 Weedon Grossmith, *From Studio to Stage* p.4
31 Marshall P Wilder, *The People I've Smiled With* pp.76-77
32 Ibid. p.77

33   See Andrew Prescott, 'Brother Irving: Sir Henry Irving and Freemasonry'. This article is reproduced on the web site of the Irving Society p.6 www.theirvingsociety.org.uk/brother_irving.htm

34   Ibid. p.1

35   Ibid. p.1 Prescott points out that freemasonry helped to erode social distinctions and to enhance prestige.

36   Sala, George Augustus *Twice Around the Clock* p.213

37   Max Pemberton, *Sixty years Ago and After* p.98

38   See Dickens, *My Early Times* p.110

39   Tony Joseph p.36

40   Charles Dickens, 'The Metropolitan Protectives' in *Hunted Down* p.103

41   Charles Dickens, *Oliver Twist* p.69

42   Montagu Williams, *Leaves of a Life* pp.144-145

43   George Augustus Sala, *Twice Around the Clock* pp.216-7

44   'The Young men in Women's Clothes' *The Times* May 16 1870 p.13

45   Ibid. p.13

46   ASC p.5

47   For a full account of the case, see Barrie Charles, *Kill the Queen* pp.102-106

48   See ASC p.5

49   ASC p.6

50   Judith Flanders, *Consuming Passions* p.361

51   ASC p.9

52   Ibid. p.9

53   Ibid. p. 9

54   Edward Walford, Old and New London 1878 (online: British History Online, Chapter XXXIV) Seethe bibliography. Walford took over from Thornbury on the project (see note 18 above)

55   *The Morning Post* December 7 1861 p.5

56   *The Morning Post* December 25 1866 p. 5

57   ASC p.14

58   *The Times* April 2 1858 p.7

59   Paul attracted attention in the national press during my research, being featured in *The Daily Mail* Jan. 22, 2013, and a query prompted a long response from Max Tyler, of the British Music Hall Society.

60   Quoted in Tony Joseph, *George Grossmith* p.51

61   *Old and New London* Vol. 5 p. 260

62   ASC p. 15 Grossmith provides a full account of the reading.

63   See 'A Chat with Mr Coney Grain, the Popular Entertainer at Home' *The Sketch* March 24 1893 p. 214

64   Hesketh Pearson, *Edward VII* p. 154

65   Charles William Day. Quoted in 'Victorian Pastimes' at www.

angelpig.net/victorian/pastimes.org

66   ASC p. 20

67   Beth Palmer, 'Florence Marryat on Page and on Stage' p. 2

68   See Tony Joseph *George Grossmith* p.63

69   Interestingly, it is listed, along with *Bric a Brac* and *Under Cover,* in *The Stage Cyclopaedia* in 1909. We can assume that all three were fairly often performed, as useful curtain-raisers, at that time.

70   J W MacQueen-Pope *Carriages at Eleven* p.23

71   Quoted in Tony Joseph *George Grossmith* p.63

72   Florence Marryat, *Tiddler's Ground* p.59

73   ACC p.21

74   *London Society* February 1874 p.120

75   ASC p.22

76   Quoted in ASC p.22

77   Peter Gammond, *Offenbach* p. 84

78   Interview, quoted in Andrew Crowther, *Gilbert of Gilbert and Sullivan* p.130

79   For instance, in 1869 there had been the case of the Welsh Fasting Girl, in which the men of science had to confront and investigate claims of a young girl's apparent survival for several months on no food or sustaining drink. Older people would have recalled the notorious case of William Dove in 1857, who was led to murder by a local 'wise man.'

80   ASC p.23

81   Ibid. p.23

82   Ibid. p.23

83   Rutland Barrington, *Rutland Barrington by Himself* p.16

84   Gilbert and Sullivan, *The Sorcerer* p.44

85   ASC p.25 Several actors commented on this. Gilbert's rather combative, military approach to life is expressed in everything. He was a perfectionist, and also enjoyed total control.

86   Leslie Baily, *The Gilbert and Sullivan Book* p.119

87   *The Times* November 19 1877

88   ASC p.27

89   Horace G Hutchinson, *Portrait of the Eighties* p.268

90   George Grossmith Jun. *GG* p.14

91   Charles Eyre Pascoe, *The Dramatic List* p.162

92   George Power, interviewed in *The Era* July 18, 1908 p.15

93   Jessie Bond, *The Life and Reminiscences of Jessie Bond* p.2 Chap. 4

94   Quoted in Leslie Baily *The Gilbert and Sullivan Book* p.136

95   *The Times* Police reports, August 16 1879 p.12

96   Tony Joseph George Grossmith p. 81. As Joseph points out, 'Why he should have been considered a suitable person to comment on those Op.Com drains remains a minor Gilbert and Sullivan mystery.'

97   Quoted in Victor Bonham Carter *Authors by Profession* p.98

98   Ibid. p.125

99   Leslie Baily *The Gilbert and Sullivan Book* p. 152

100   ASC p.28

101   Joseph Lehmann, *All Sir Garnet: A life of Field Marshall Sir Garnet Wolseley* p.159

102   Ibid. p.166

103   Law report, *The Times* May 28 1880 p.12

104   Ibid. p.12

105   Tony Joseph p.84

106   ASC p.29

107   Letter quoted in Tony Joseph p.85

108   Quoted in Leslie Baily *The Gilbert and Sullivan Book* pp.171-172

109   See, for instance, the long article on 'The Stage in 1878' in *The Times* for January 16 1879, which glosses briefly *Pinafore* and then spends much more column space on Gilbert's other work.

110   Review: *The Era* August 1 1880 issue 2184

111   *The Examiner* August 14 1880 issue 3785 The writer generally appears to appreciate the dramatic form before him, but insists on adding ambiguous phrase to judgement which on the surface appear to be positive ones.

112   Janet Snowman, *John Orlando Parry and the Theatre of London* pp.140-141

113   George Grossmith Junior *GG* pp.11-12

114   Harry Furniss, *My Bohemian Days* p.158

115   Richard Ellmann, *Oscar Wilde* p.126

116   Ibid. p.128

117   Quoted ibid. p.129

118   ASC p.30

119   *The Pall Mall Gazette* April 25, 1881 issue 5044

120   *The Era* April 30 1881 p. 12

121   George Grossmith Jun. *GG* pp.232-233

122   Robert Blake *D'Israeli* p.115

123   Ibid. p.115

124   *Hansard* May 6 1879 Vol. 245 p.1789

125   Ibid. p.1790

126   Hawkins, Sir Henry, *Reminiscences* p.344

127   The diary of Henry Spencer Ashbee, quoted in James Agate, *Ego 9* p.291 Ashbee was a member of the philoerotica group, which included the great explorer and spy, Sir Richard Burton. He is reckoned to be the author of *My Secret Life* but this is not fully verified.

128   Such burlesques had elements very similar to comic opera. In the case of Bombastes, the setting would have pleased Gilbert: Utopia.

129   Hudson, Derek, notes to *Princess Ida* p.288

130   Tennyson, 'The Princess' *Collected Poems* p.167

131   Letter from Sullivan to Gilbert, quoted in Leslie Baily p.233.

132   This is reported, and the feature reproduced in full, in James Agate's *Those Were the Nights* p. 39

133   *Princess Ida* Act I p.2

134   Andrew Crowther, *Gilbert of Gilbert and Sullivan* p.173

135   Letter from Sullivan to Gilbert quoted ibid. p.236

136   Soldene, Emily, *My Theatrical and Musical Recollections* p.90

137   *GG* p.11

138   *The Era* September 7 1884 quoted in Joseph p.106

139   ASC p.30

140   Quoted in Leslie Baily, *The Gilbert and Sullivan Book* p.245

141   Quoted in Tony Joseph p.110

142   The exhibition was in Humphrey's Hall, between 1885 and 1887. In May 1885 the hall was destroyed in a fire and man died. But it was rebuilt. Gilbert had written Act One around two months before the exhibition opened, so it was not a direct influence. Gilbert, quite simply, was acutely responsive to trends and fads in the arts and culture. *The Mikado* was arguably his most notable success in this respect.

143   Derek Hudson, introduction to *Ruddigore* p.69

144   Both quoted in Tony Joseph p.113

145   'Playgoer' *Penny Illustrated Paper* January 29 1887 p.74

146   Leslie Baily, *The Gilbert and Sullivan Book* p.270

147   Tony Joseph, *George Grossmith* p.115

148   'Ruddy George at Toole's' *The Era* March 26, 1887 issue 2531

149   Ibid. (Following on from previous reference, same page)

150   Frank Archer, *An Actor's Notebooks* p.295

151   'Mr George Grossmith at Colchester' *The Essex Standard* April 23, 1887 p.5

152   See for instance, in Hesketh Pearson, Edward VII p. 112: ' He staked his gold upon the chances of a Card or the roll of a ball – gold, be it remembered from the toil and sweat of the British working Man...' (Reference to *Reynolds's Newspaper*.)

153   'An Old Savoyard' *The Times* July 26 1922 p.7

154   Tony Joseph, *George Grossmith* p.124

155   Letter quoted in Leslie Baily, *The Gilbert and Sullivan Book* p.307

156   'The Society Clown at Home' *The Graphic* June 26 1890 p.18

157   ASC p.30

158   Letter from Corney Grain to Mrs Robertson May 29 1889

159   Michael Kilgarriff, *The Golden Age of Melodrama* p.397

160   William Archer, *Real Conversations* p.129

161   Peter Bailey, *Music Hall, The Business of Pleasure* p.96

162 Harold Scott, *The Early Doors* p.188

163 Ibid. p.188

164 Robert Keith Middleton, *The Master Builders* pp.131-132

165 ASC p.34

166 ASC p.34

167 'Mr Nelson Jackson' obituary *The Times* May 15 1951 p.6

168 ' Mr Grossmith and his Piano' *Pall Mall Gazette* 1888 Reproduced at www.paperspast.natlib.govt.nz p.4

169 Ibid p.1

170 J Hickory Wood, *Dan Leno* p.41

171 ASC p.31

172 Ibid. p.33

173 James Agate, *Ego 2* p.382

174 Gervase Hughes, *Composers of Operetta* (London: Macmillan, 1962)

175 F E Marshall Steel, *The Encore Reciter* p.x

176 ASC p.42

177 Christopher Fifield, *Ibbs and Tillett: The Rise and Fall of a Musical Empire* p.9

178 Tony Joseph, *George Grossmith* p. 134.

179 Quoted ibid. p.135

180 Charles Greville, *Diary* p.274

181 Elizabeth Longford, *Victoria R.I.* p.510

182 Ibid p.510. Longford also writes: ' A gramophone was brought to Balmoral by Mr Morse And after the household had recorded whistles and German jokes, Her Majesty spoke a few Words.' Ibid.

183 'Alleged Bogus Theatrical Agency' *The Times* August 31 1898 p.9

184 W S Gilbert, *Haste to the Wedding* in *Eight Original Comic Operas* p.24

185 Review quoted in Tony Joseph, *George Grossmith* p.146

186 'The Society Clown as a Composer' *Pall Mall Gazette* February 4 1892 issue 8385

187 Review in *The Era* July 30, 1892 issue 2810

188 Letter quoted in Tony Joseph, *George Grossmith* p. 150

189 Joseph Roach, 'Public Intimacy: The Prior History of "It" in Luckhurst and Moody, *Theatre and Celebrity in Britain 1660-2000* p. 24

190 *Dan Leno* p.69

191 Dr Andrew Prescott, 'A History of British Freemasonry 1425-2000 at www.freemasons-freemasonry.com/prescott16.html

192 Paula Gillett, *The Victorian Painter's World* p.123

193 The New Vagabonds' Club *The Times* Dec.11 1897 p.13

194 St George's Hall *The Times* December 27 1898 p.5

195 'Mark Twain: Guest of the Vagabonds' *West Gippsland Gazette* August 29 1899 p.3

196 The Society Clown at Home *The Daily Graphic* June 28, 1890 p.12

197 ASC p.4

198 Quoted in Tony Joseph, *George Grossmith* p. 43

199 *The Era* June 9 1900 p. 14

200 Letter from Weedon to Mrs Tweedie May 29 1894 (author's collection).

201 James Agate, *Buzz Buzz!* P.p. 161-162

202 *The Stage* June 6 1895 p.9

203 Gissing, quoted in Dehn Gilmore in Phillips, *A Mighty Mass of Brick and Smoke* p.156

204 'Mr J W Arrowsmith, Bristol Publisher' *The Sketch* September 11 1895 p.371

205 Ibid. p.371

206 See Eugene Byrne's blog, eugenebyrne.wordpress.com/2011/01/16called-back1883

207 Charles Greville *Diary* p.8

208 C H Rolph, *London Particulars* p.156

209 'Lanes and Field paths near London' *The Times* October 10 1887 p.3

210 'Health of City Clerks' *The Times* August 20 1913 p.2

211 Lynne Hapgood, *Margins of Desire* p.222

212 Ibid. p.190

213 *The Diary of a Nobody* p.185

214 'A Speculator's Action' *The Times* June 23 1891 p.3

215 *The Diary of a Nobody* p.44

216 Richard Jefferies, *The Story of My Heart* pp.61-62

217 Somerset Maugham, *A Writer's Notebook* p.32

218 *The Diary of a Nobody* p.22

219 Richard Church, *The Voyage Home* epigraph p.5

220 Ibid. p.10

221 J C Squire, introduction to *The Diary of a Nobody* (1924 edition) p.7

222 Clarence Cook, *House Beautiful* p.20

223 *The Diary of a Nobody* p.7

224 Ibid. p.34

225 Ibid. p.44

226 Tony Joseph, *George Grossmith* p.167

227 Reviews: *The Morning Post* July 20 1892 p.3

228 *The Pall Mall Gazette* Publishers' announcements July 26 1892 issue 8532

229 Quoted in the *Diary* 1924 edition Advertisement

230 Tony Joseph, *George Grossmith* p.181

231 *The Times* review, quoted in Kurt Ganzl, *The British Musical Theatre* p.736

232 Ibid. p.736

233 Referee review, quoted in Tony Joseph, *George Grossmith* p.181

234 Quoted in Tony Joseph, *George Grossmith* p.176

235 'The Last Night of the First Gaiety' *The Times* July 12 1961 p.12

236 B C Hilliam 'How the Dying Irving Helped Grossmith' *The Times* October 12 1962 p.14

237 Ibid. p.14

238 Ibid. p.14

239 'Did He?' *Penny Illustrated Paper* May 25 1912 p.650

240 For an account of the dinner, see Andrew Crowther, *Gilbert of Gilbert and Sullivan* p.227

241 *Diary of a Nobody* p.191

242 The photo is in *GG* p.16

243 'Mr George Grossmith at Folkestone' *Folkestone Express* April 13 1901

244 'Woodward Institute' *Folkestone Herald* January 29 1910

245 Obituary, *Folkestone Herald* March 2 1912

246 Ibid.

247 ibid

248 Ibid.

249 Report in *The Brighton Gazette* quoted in Tony Joseph, *George Grossmith* p. 194

250 Somerset Maugham, *A Writer's Notebook* p.53

251 Stanley Naylor, *Gaity and George Grossmith* p.9

252 George Grossmith Jnr *GG* p.40

253 Review in *The Era* May 5 1900

254 Review in *The Era* August 10 1907

255 Duke of York's Theatre *The Times* March 14 1904 p.8

256 Quote from *The Queen* magazine, used in Elston's brochure

257 'The World of Women' *Bury and Norwich Post and Suffolk Standard* October 23 1900 p.7

258 *The Star,* Sydney April 6, 1898 text online at www.paperspast.natlib. govt.nz/cgi